A Burning and a Shining Light

A Profile of John the Baptist

Paul G. Koch

Legacy of Words
La Crosse, IN 46348

A BURNING AND A SHINING LIGHT
A Profile of John the Baptist

Library of Congress Card 96-077100
Legacy of Words
117 Vermont St
La Crosse IN
Published 1996
Printed in the United States of America,
Morris Publishing, Kearney, NE
ISBN 0-9644799-3-1

Table of Contents

Dedicated to All Faithful Preachers of the Gospel

Foreword

After our Lord, there is no greater example (role model) for a Christian than John the Baptist. Jesus Himself gave him the singular commendation, "He was a burning and a shining light" (John 5:35). Moreover, the ultimate purpose of John's life was to give all glory to Jesus. A disciple of the Savior today cannot choose a better motto for his life than John expressed, "He must increase, but I must decrease" (John 3:30). Jesus gave the measure of the Forerunner's stature when He declared, "Among those that are born of women there is not a greater prophet than John the Baptist" (Luke 7:28; cf. Matt. 11:11).

Because the example of John the Baptist is particularly relevant for ministers of the Gospel, I have devoted Chapter XV to the theme, *John the Baptist, A Pattern For Preachers*.

The reason for presenting this book as a profile of John the Baptist is that no comprehensive study of the great prophet, relying upon the Gospels as truthful history, has been published in recent years. A Scriptural appraisal of the questions raised in our time regarding the source of John's teachings and baptism is needed. I have considered it apropos also to discuss the doctrinal implications of John's ministry with reference to the *corpus doctrinae* (the body of doctrine) of the New Testament.

A subject which has engaged the recent research of scholars has been considered in Chapter IX, *John the Baptist and the Essenes*. A perennial question has, I believe, been answered satisfactorily in

Chapter XII, *Did John Doubt Jesus' Messiahship?*

Numerous pages have been reserved to consider the influence which Christ's Forerunner has even today in the worship of the liturgical churches. Similarly, space has been given to the influence he has had outside Christendom.

Several chapters delineate how poetry, music, drama, and iconography reflect the life and mission of John the Baptist. Separate pages reproducing works of art have been included for illustrating the symbols related to the Forerunner's work and to give examples of artistic license.

The author regards the canonical Scriptures of the Old and New Testaments in all their words and thoughts to be the inerrant Word of God, given by inspiration of the Holy Spirit. He accepts what the Bible says about the life and work of the Forerunner as the absolute truth.

The exposition of the Scripture passages relative to John the Baptist is based upon the Hebrew and Greek texts. I have quoted the *King James Version* (except in a few instances) because of its continued acceptance and use by Bible readers. It, like *Luther's German Bible*, is a classic among the translations which have been (and continue to be) published. I have followed the spelling, capitalization, and the unique punctuation of the *King James Version*.

I have referred consistently to the Forerunner as "John the Baptist," rather than "John the Baptizer," as several recent translations name him. "John the Baptist" is the name by which English speaking people have known him for at least six hundred years. The name is part of our culture.

Some repetition of explanations will be apparent in comparing chapters. Such repetition was necessary to present a chapter as a complete unit. Please consider the chapter notes as comments which shed additional light upon what is presented in a chapter.

Since the usefulness of a book is enhanced for reference by a comprehensive index, a listing of all Bible passages quoted or noted has been given, and an index of names and subjects.

SOLI DEO GLORIA

Paul G. Koch

O N E

The Advent of John the Baptist in Prophecy

There are three prophecies of the coming of John the Forerunner of Christ recorded in the Old Testament. They are: Isaiah 40:1-8, Malachi 3:1, and Malachi 4:5.

The Prophecy of Isaiah

"Comfort ye, comfort ye my people, saith your God. Speak ye comfortably to Jerusalem, and cry unto her, that her warfare is accomplished, that her iniquity is pardoned: for she hath received of the Lord's hand double for all her sins. The voice of him that crieth in the wilderness. Prepare ye the way of the Lord, make straight in the desert a highway for our God. Every valley shall be exalted, and every mountain and hill shall be made low: and the crooked shall be made straight, and the rough places plain: And the glory of the Lord shall be revealed and all flesh shall see it together: for the mouth of the Lord hath spoken it. The voice said, Cry. And he said, What shall I cry? All flesh is grass, and all the goodliness thereof is as the flower of the field: The grass withereth, the flower fadeth: because the spirit of the Lord bloweth upon it: surely the people is grass. The grass withereth, the flower fadeth: but the word of our God shall stand forever."

The prophecy begins with a general directive to dispense comfort to God's people.[1] The comfort which is to be given is the most needed and the most consoling which can be spoken, namely, the pronouncement that the state of warfare between God and sinners has been ended,[2] that their iniquities have been forgiven, and that there is ample forgiveness with the Lord.[3] This message is the basis for the ministry of all God's messengers, although here it is prophetic of John the Baptist.

The voice in the wilderness tells the people to prepare the way of the Lord under the imagery of the preparations which would be made to receive an oriental monarch. The road improvements are to be carried out for easy access. The work is to be done to honor the monarch and to show that his coming is welcomed. Of course, the imagery of these preparations is not to be taken literally, but in a spiritual sense. That is, every spiritual barrier of sin should be removed by repentance. Sin hinders, yes prevents, the advent of the Lord. And it is the way of the **Lord** and the highway of our **God** which are to be ready when He comes.

The results of the advent of the Lord are that the glory of the Lord shall be revealed, and all flesh will recognize that God has come to His people.

More than one voice is indicated in Isaiah 40:6. The voice which calls, "Cry," is not identified. Evidently it is the Lord issuing a command. The voice which asks, "What shall I cry?" is the voice in the wilderness of verse 3. The message which is to be proclaimed is a melancholy one, "All flesh is grass." But, in contrast to this sad statement the voice is to say, "The word of our God shall stand forever." The significance of this heartening pronouncement is given in 1 Peter 1:24, 25. There is the quotation from Isaiah 40:6 regarding human frailty, and then the statements: "But the word of the Lord endureth forever. And this is the word which by the gospel is preached unto you." That word of the Gospel is the comfort which the voice and all other spokesmen for the Lord are to proclaim by telling sinful, frail human beings that their warfare has ended, and that their sins have been forgiven.

The New Testament Fulfillment of Isaiah 40

Matthew 3:1-3: "In those days came John the Baptist, preaching in the wilderness of Judea, and saying, Repent ye: for the kingdom of heaven is at hand. For this is he that was

8

spoken of the prophet Esaias, saying, **The voice of one crying in the wilderness, Prepare ye the way of the Lord, make his paths straight."**

Mark 1:3: **"The voice of one crying in the wilderness, Prepare ye the way of the Lord, make his paths straight."**

Luke 1:76-79: "And thou child, shalt be called the prophet of the Highest: for **thou shalt go before the face of the Lord to prepare his ways; To give knowledge of salvation unto his people by the remission of their sins.** Through the tender mercy of our God; whereby the dayspring from on high hath visited us, To give light to them that sit in darkness and in the shadow of death, to guide our feet into the way of peace."

Luke 3:3-6: "And he came into all the country about Jordan, preaching the baptism of repentance for the remission of sins; As it is written in the book of the words of Esaias the prophet, saying, **The voice of one crying in the wilderness, Prepare ye the way of the Lord, make his paths straight. Every valley shall be filled, and every mountain and hill shall be brought low; and the crooked shall be made straight, and the rough ways shall be made smooth; And all flesh shall see the salvation of God."**

John 1:23: "He said, **I am the voice of one crying in the wilderness, Make straight the way of the Lord,** as said the prophet Esaias."

John 1:29: "The next day John seeth Jesus coming and saith, **Behold the Lamb of God, which taketh away the sin of the world."**[4]

The Prophecies of Malachi

There are two passage in the book of the prophet Malachi which foretell the coming of the Savior's Forerunner, John the Baptist.

Malachi 3:1 "Behold, I will send my messenger,[5] and he shall prepare the way before me: and the Lord, whom ye seek, shall suddenly come to his temple,[6] even the messenger of the covenant,[7] whom ye delight in: behold, he shall come, saith the Lord of hosts."

Malachi 4:5, 6: "Behold, I will send you Elijah the prophet before the coming of the great and dreadful day of the Lord: And he shall turn the heart of the fathers to the children, and the heart of the children to their fathers, lest I come and smite the earth with a curse."

The New Testament Fulfillment

Matthew 11:10, 14: "For this is he, of whom it is written, **Behold I send my messenger before thy face, which shall prepare thy way before thee. . .**And if ye will receive it, **this is Elias, which was for to come.**"

Luke 1:17: "And **he shall go before him in the spirit and power of Elias, to turn the hearts of the fathers to the children,** and the disobedient to the wisdom of the just; **to make ready a people prepared for the Lord.**"[8]

Mark 1:2: "As it is written in the prophets, **Behold, I send my messenger before thy face, which shall prepare thy way before thee.**"

Chapter Notes

1. Jerusalem = the Church, God's people.
2. "Warfare" is a literal translation. Most interpreters take this in a figurative sense, e.g., Jennings, F.C., *Studies in Isaiah,* Neptune, New Jersey, Loizeaux Brothers, 1966, p. 461, "trouble." We believe that Kenneth K. Miller correctly explains: "God is no longer at war with us, because our offenses have been removed. Sin makes God our enemy, but Paul writes, 'When we were enemies, we were reconciled to God by the death of his Son.' God has declared peace with us, 'Peace on earth, good will toward men.'" (Miller, Kenneth K., *The Gospel According to Isaiah,* Ann Arbor, Cushing-Malley, 1992, p. 237.)
3. Cf. Romans 5:20: "Where sin abounded, grace did much more abound."
4. Please note that these verses reveal the content of John's preaching as both Law and Gospel. See our Chapter, *John the Baptist's Message* for a discussion of his preaching.
5. The messenger who is sent is identified in the New Testament as John the Baptist (Mark 1:2).
6. "His temple" does not refer to the Temple in Jerusalem, but to God's people (the Church = the total number of believers) in whom God dwells individually and collectively (1 Cor. 3:16, 17; 2 Cor. 6:16).
7. "The messenger of the covenant" is Christ, who in the Old Testament appeared as the Angel (Messenger) of the Lord. See

10

Laetsch, Theo., *The Minor Prophets*, St. Louis, Concordia, 1956, p. 409f, for a comprehensive article about Christ before His incarnation.

8. See our Chapter, *The Birth of John the Baptist*, for comments on these words of the Angel Gabriel.

T W O

The Parents
of John the Baptist

All that is revealed in the Bible about Zacharias and Elisabeth, the parents of John the Baptist, is recorded in St. Luke, Chapter One. Immediately after the prolog, verses 1-4, the Evangelist introduces the aged couple as living at the time of Herod the King of Judea.[1]

Zacharias was a priest who lived in the hill country of Judea (v. 39) south of Jerusalem. What is told about his character and faith distinguishes him from the priests who were his contemporaries. At the time of King David the descendants of Aaron were divided into twenty-four courses. Each of the courses ministered in the Temple one week. Zacharias was of the course of Abia, the eighth division of priests. It was his lot to burn incense the week of his service, a distinct honor which would occur once in a lifetime.[2] Elisabeth, his wife, was also a descendant of Aaron (Luke 1:5).

Zacharias and Elisabeth are described as being righteous before God. This refers to their standing as saints in God's sight through faith in the promised Messiah. Elisabeth's words of greeting to Mary (vv. 41-45) are a confession of faith in her Lord. Likewise, *The Benedictus* of Zacharias, delivered at the circumcision of John, is a confession of faith in the remission of sins and in the Messiah of Israel.

The words "walking in all the commandments and ordinances of the Lord blameless" (v. 6) are a statement regarding their devout lives and sanctification.

Both Elisabeth and Zacharias were filled with the Holy Ghost (Luke

1:41-45; 67-79) and spoke inspired words. These words should be regarded as true and inerrant as compared with other utterances to which they gave expression. Elisabeth spoke by inspiration of the Holy Spirit when the Virgin Mary came to visit her (Luke 1:41). Zacharias spoke by the Holy Spirit when he praised God in *The Benedictus* (Luke 1:67).

Zacharias and Elisabeth are described as childless - for two reasons: Elisabeth was barren, and both she and her husband were past the age when people can have children (Luke 1:7). That they were without children was a grievous burden for the devout couple. Elisabeth considered it a reproach among her people to be childless. When she, therefore, knew that she was with child, she expressed her joy, saying, "Thus hath the Lord dealt with me in the days wherein he looked on me, to take away my reproach among men" (Luke 1:25).

The only blot upon the character of Zacharias exposed in the narrative of St. Luke is that he doubted the good news told by the Angel Gabriel and asked for a sign to confirm his message. He said, "Whereby shall I know this? for I am an old man, and my wife well stricken in years" (Luke 1:18). Consequently, he was deprived of speech immediately and all during the nine months of Elisabeth's pregnancy.

Zacharias, nevertheless, communicated to his spouse, most likely in writing, what the Angel Gabriel had said, so that they were in agreement on the day of circumcision that their son should be called John.[3]

It must be said to the credit of Zacharias that he completed the days of his ministry in the Temple before returning home.

The Evangelist Luke does not tell for how long a time the child of Zacharias and Elisabeth had the blessing of the wholesome guidance and example of his parents. Since they were advanced in years, it may be that they died before he grew to manhood. (He was about thirty years of age when he began his ministry in the wilderness of Judea.)[4] God somehow provided for John's earthly needs and his nurture in the Lord during his maturing years.[5]

Chapter Notes

1. Herod the Great (died 4 B.C.) ruled over all of Palestine. He was called "the Great" because of his extensive building projects.
2. Edersheim, Alfred, *The Life and Times of Jesus the Messiah*, Grand Rapids, Eerdmans, 1886, Vol. I, p.134.
3. There is also the possibility that the Holy Spirit gave Elisabeth a

direct revelation and command that the boy should be called John.
4. Cf. Luke 3:1, 2 and 3:23.
5. Some scholars have speculated that John may have been reared in the Qumran community. It is unlikely that the son of an orthodox priest was placed into such a spiritual environment. Also, scholars, after considered comparisons, have concluded that John's preaching and baptism have no affinity with the religion of the Essenes. See our Chapter, *John the Baptist and the Essenes*.

THREE

The Birth
of John the Baptist

The people of the hill country of Judea who heard about the wondrous happenings related to the birth of John the Forerunner asked, "What manner of child shall this be?" And truly, the circumstances of his birth presaged the life and career of an extraordinary personage. Consider the following:

1. His coming had been prophesied in Isaiah 40:1-8 and in Malachi 3:1 and 4:5;

2. His birth was foretold by an angel, Luke 1:11-20. This prophecy of Gabriel described John's marvelous destiny;

3. His name was given by the angel before he was born, Luke 1:13;

4. His birth was an answer to prayer, Luke 1:13;

5. He was conceived when his parents were beyond years and of a mother who had been barren, Luke 1:7, 18, 25;

6. John was filled with the Holy Ghost from his mother's womb, Luke 1:15, 41, 44;

7. John's father was given a sign; he was unable to speak from the time that the Angel Gabriel announced the child's birth until the day of the circumcision.

The Annunciation

Zacharias's lot as a priest was to burn incense at the Temple in Jerusalem. As he carried out this function of his office, the Angel

Gabriel, standing on the right side of the altar of incense, appeared to him. Since it was the time when the people were gathered for prayer, some scholars have concluded that it was at the time of the evening sacrifice that this appearance occurred.[1]

That Zacharias was troubled and fearful at the sight of the angel is not surprising. Sinful human beings confronted by that which is holy and heavenly are stricken with fear. (Compare the Bethlehem shepherds, Luke 2:9.) The Angel Gabriel assured the priest, "Fear not, Zacharias: for thy prayer is heard." The prayer to which the angel referred was evidently the petition for a child, which had been in Zacharias's prayers down through the years. This petition probably had not been voiced in recent years, considering his reaction of disbelief.[2]

The angel told Zacharias that Elisabeth would bear him a son, and that he should call him John ("Jehovah is gracious"). This name was especially fitting because of the miraculous nature of his conception. The angel declared that not only Zacharias would have joy and gladness, but that many people would rejoice at the child's birth. John would be great in the sight of the Lord (as contrasted with persons who are considered great in the sight of men).[3]

The prophecy that John would drink neither wine nor strong drink meant that he would be a life-long Nazarite, as Samuel and Samson were.[4]

The most surprising statement of Gabriel, theologically considered, is that John the Baptist was to be filled with the Holy Ghost "even from his mother's womb." Does this mean from the moment of conception, i.e. at the beginning of life? The Scripture does not say. However, in the sixth month of his mother's pregnancy, when the Virgin Mary, pregnant with the Son of God, spoke her greeting, the child in Elisabeth's womb leaped for joy, Luke 1:41, 44. A valid theological conclusion is that, though the Holy Spirit ordinarily comes to a child (or adult) through Holy Baptism,[5] God is not restricted to the Means of Grace, but can work faith and bestow the Holy Spirit even to an unborn child.

Last of all, the Angel Gabriel spoke about the mission of John the Forerunner. He would turn many of the children of Israel to the Lord their God. The Holy Spirit would bring about the conversion of many in Israel through the ministry of John the Baptist.

John was to precede the Lord with the same spiritual endowments as the Prophet Elijah and with the power inherent within the Word of God, bringing his hearers about to repentance. He would turn the hearts of the fathers and the hearts of their children, so that the "generation gap" would be bridged by a common understanding in their attitude toward the Lord. Those who because of their unbelief are disobedient will be turned about to the wisdom of those justified by faith. These words of Gabriel describe the spiritual results which would be brought about through the ministry of John the Baptist. His mission was to make a people prepared for the Lord.

Zacharias's Unbelief

Zacharias did not believe what he heard. His unbelief was based upon circumstances as they were. He was an old man, and his wife was well stricken in years. He sought a sign from the angel to confirm the promise that had been given.

The Angel Gabriel answered Zacharias's unbelief by asserting: "I am Gabriel that stand in the presence of God. . ."[6] It is impossible for an angelic being who stands in the presence of a holy God to lie. Zacharias should have believed the angel's good tidings. The unbelieving priest is granted a sign indeed, one that will rebuke him every day until there is a fulfillment of the prophecy. He will be dumb, that is, unable to speak, until the day that the angel's words will be fulfilled.

The people at worship in the Temple waited for Zacharias to appear, wondering, no doubt, why it was taking him so long to perform the task of incensing. When he appeared, he was unable to speak the words of the customary blessing, but beckoned to them that they should depart. The people (with remarkable perception) concluded that he had received a vision.

Zacharias completed the days of his ministration. He performed the functions of his office as best he could under the handicap of being unable to speak. Possibly, in the days which followed, one of his fellow priests assumed the role of speaking for him those parts of the service which required speaking.

The conception of the child John the Baptist happened soon after Zacharias returned home from his ministry in the Temple. Elisabeth stayed at home and did not appear in public. This was, no doubt, the ordinary conduct of a woman with child of that time and culture. Joyfully and thankfully she said, "Thus hath the Lord dealt with me in the days wherein he looked on me, to take away my reproach among men" (Luke 1:25).

The Virgin Mary Visits Elisabeth

The fifth month of Elisabeth's confinement[7] is mentioned because in the sixth month the Virgin Mary was prompted to visit Elisabeth, for the Angel Gabriel had told her that her "cousin"[8] in her old age had conceived. Mary would feel a special affinity for her kinswoman under the similar circumstances. As soon as Mary entered the house of Zacharias, located in the hill country of Judea, and greeted Elisabeth, the child John the Baptist leaped in her womb, and she was filled with the Holy Ghost. The words spoken were no ordinary thoughts, but were words given (inspired) by the Holy Spirit. Elisabeth said in a loud voice, "Blessed art thou among women, and blessed is the fruit of thy womb. And whence is this to me, that the mother of my Lord should come to me? For, lo, as soon as the voice of thy salutation sounded in mine ears, the babe leaped in my womb for joy. And blessed is she that believed: for there shall be a performance of those things which were told her from the Lord" (Luke 1:42-45). Mary's response to Elisabeth's inspired words was a beautiful confession of faith, known as *The Magnificat*.[9]

Mary remained with Elisabeth for a visit of approximately three months and returned to Nazareth shortly before the birth of John the Baptist.

The Child Named John

The child promised by the Angel Gabriel was born to the aged couple as foretold. The neighbors and relatives recognized the mercy of God in giving a son to Elisabeth who had been barren, and they rejoiced with her. They came to be present for the circumcision of the child on the eighth day. They were calling him Zacharias[10] after his father as they talked. His mother objected to this and said, "Not so; but he shall be called John." Apparently, the time of the circumcision was the occasion for naming a male child (Cf. Luke 2:21). The neighbors and relatives persisted and said, "There is none of thy kindred that is called by this name" (Luke 1:61). They then made signs to his father to ask him what he would have him called.[11] Zacharias beckoned for a writing table, and to the wonderment of those who were present wrote, "His name is John." Having written these words, he at once began to speak and to praise God. His words of praise were, no doubt, those which St. Luke has inserted after the sentences in verses 65 and 66.

These words of *The Benedictus*,[12] delivered under the inspiration of the Holy Spirit, are considered in a separate chapter which follows.

A climate of awe surrounded the house of Zacharias and Elizabeth. The sayings of Zacharias[13] were the subject of repetition and rumor throughout the hill country. All that heard these sayings were asking, "What manner of child shall this be?"

The further Scripture notations regarding the childhood of John the Baptist are meager in substance. Luke 1:66b gives us the terse statement, "And the hand of the Lord was with him." Luke 1:80 gives the summation of all the years from John's infancy until the time he began to preach in the wilderness of Judea at the age of thirty: "And the child grew, and waxed strong in spirit, and was in the deserts till the day of his shewing to Israel." The statement that John waxed strong in spirit has reference to his religious life and spiritual development.

The Gospels do not give information as to whether John's parents had the joy of seeing him grow to manhood. The words regarding his being in the deserts until the day he began his ministry to Israel suggest that he studied and gave himself to meditation in solitude in the years which preceded his clarion call, "Repent ye; for the kingdom of heaven is at hand" (Matt. 3:2).

Chapter Notes

1. Edersheim, Alfred, *The Life and Times of Jesus the Messiah*, Grand Rapids, Eerdmans, 1886, Vol. I, p.133, presumes that Zacharias's ministry was performed "in the morning, as the principal service." The time of the worship cannot be established with certainty.

2. Since the birth of the child was related to the Messianic hope, the prayers of Zacharias in anticipation of Christ's coming were heard and also the earlier supplications for a child.

3. Cf. Jesus' statement that there was no one born greater than John the Baptist (Matt. 11:11; Luke 7:28).

4. See Numbers 6:1-21 for the law of the Nazarite.

5. Cf. John 3:5; Acts 2:38; Titus 3:5.

6. Cf. Matt. 18:10.

7. Luke 1:24.

8. *suggenis* means "kinswoman," "female relative." The Greek word does not indicate the exact relationship.

9. Arndt, William, *Bible Commentary St. Luke*, St. Louis, Concordia, 1956, pp. 52 & 62, assumes that Mary's *The Magnificat* also was

inspired by the Holy Spirit. This cannot be asserted with certainty because it is not stated in the sacred record.

10. *ekaloun* is a conative imperfect tense. It expresses the attempt to have the boy named after his father.

11. Some scholars think that the gestures made to ask the opinion of Zacharias show that he was stricken with deafness as well as being mute. Gabriel's words in Luke 1:20 regarding the chastisement do not say this. (The people may have treated him as if he were a deaf-mute.)

12. The poetic prayer of praise spoken by Zacharias (by the inspiration of the Holy Spirit) is called *The Benedictus* because of the first word of the Latin version.

13. The singular statements in *The Benedictus* would be remembered and evaluated as to their fulfillment.

FOUR

The Benedictus

Zacharias was deprived of the gift of speech during the nine months of Elisabeth's confinement. This was the chastisement, because of his unbelief, which the Angel Gabriel had foretold. Zacharias had no reason for doubting the heavenly messenger who came to him in the sacred precincts of the Temple as he served in his holy office. Moreover, there was the singular birth of Isaac to Abraham and Sarah in their old age. Zacharias should have been mindful of this and of other instances recorded in the Old Testament of the Lord opening the womb.

At the circumcision of Zacharias's son, when the name was to be given, according to the Jewish custom,[1] he was asked by means of signs about his choice of a name for the boy. He motioned for a "writing table" and wrote on it, "His name is John." Then, immediately, his speech was restored, so that he spoke and praised God (v. 64). Although two verses intervene in the narrative of St. Luke, in which the reaction of the people of the hill country to these remarkable happenings is recorded, what Zacharias spoke in praise of God are the poetic sentences known through the centuries as *The Benedictus*. This title is derived from the first word of the prayer in the Latin translation.

An Inspired Psalm

The Benedictus may be called a psalm because it is a prayer in the style of Hebrew poetry. This unique form of poetry, which consists of rhythmic sentences expressing repetitions of thought, is called parallelism. It is found in the ancient literature of other than Hebrew people.[2] What distinguishes the poem of Zacharias, and makes it comparable to the 150 psalms of the Psalter, is that Zacharias spoke these words by inspiration of the Holy Spirit. This means that the words and thoughts expressed by Zacharias are not his words and thoughts, but those of God the Holy Spirit, the Third Person of the blessed Trinity. Because these are divine words, they are true and reliable. What Zacharias spoke by the breathing in of the Holy Spirit is as prophetic as that which the psalmist David wrote. He declared: "The Spirit of the Lord spake by me, and his word was in my tongue" (2 Sam. 23:2). The prophetic utterance of Zacharias is the last prophecy of an Old Testament servant of God. It, however, belongs to the New Testament because of its imminent fulfillment in the ministry of John the Baptist and in the coming of the Savior whom John preceded.

A Psalm of Praise

The psalm of Zacharias begins with a doxology directed to the Lord (Jehovah) the God of Israel. The reason for this praise is that "He has visited[3] and redeemed[4] his people." (Note that he speaks of the redemption as an accomplished fact in anticipation of Christ's coming.) He says further that God has "raised up an horn of salvation for us in the house of his servant David." (Horns are used by animals for their protection. Here the horn is used as a symbol of the safety sinners have through the salvation which God has provided. Thus in Psalm 18:2 the Lord is called "the horn of my salvation.")[5] Since Jesus was of the house and lineage of David, the horn of salvation is described in *The Benedictus* as having been raised up in the house of David.

Salvation Defined

The next words of Zacharias show that God has been faithful to fulfill His Word. He has done what He promised through His holy prophets from ancient times.[6] The salvation is "from our enemies and from the hand of all that hate us." These are the same enemies described by Paul in Ephesians 6:12. These are the devil and all his cohorts, including the wicked people under his influence. "And from the hand of all that hate us" parallels "our enemies." The "hand" refers to the control which the devil and all evil forces have over persons before they have been freed from the dominion of sin.

God's Faithfulness

"To perform the mercy promised to our fathers, and to remember his holy covenant; the oath which he swore to our father Abraham . . ." The holy covenant of the Old Testament looked forward to Christ and the New Testament in His blood,[7] a covenant of mercy promised to the Israel of the Old Testament. God swore an oath to Abraham that in his Seed all the nations of the earth would be blessed. He repeated this promise to Abraham's descendants.

The "mercy" of the statement above is placed in perspective as the blessed cause of delivering those who afterward are able to serve God without fear of punishment, in righteousness and holiness before Him all the days of their lives.[8] This is the purpose of their redemption; they have been saved to serve God. Compare Ephesians 2:10: "For we are his workmanship, created in Christ Jesus unto good works, which God hath before ordained that we should walk in them."

John's Mission

Zacharias, having spoken of the great work of salvation which God is about to bring to pass, then speaks of the role which his son, John the Baptist, is to occupy in relation to God's new dispensation in Christ.

That John is to be "called" the prophet of the Highest means that *he will be* the prophet of the Highest. John's mission as the prophet of God is explained: "For thou shalt go before the face of the Lord to prepare his ways." This is exactly what God had prophesied through Isaiah in the 40th Chapter, that the Forerunner would precede the Lord and make ready a highway for our God.

The next words tell specifically how this is to be done: "To give knowledge of salvation unto his people by the remission of their sins" (v. 77). He is to give his people the assurance that their sins have been forgiven. John did this by preaching the baptism of repentance for the remission of sins and by pointing to Jesus as the Lamb of God who takes away the sin of the world. This message of forgiveness, by the working of the Holy Spirit, imparts the saving knowledge for faith in Christ.

Tender Mercy and Peace

The message of the Forerunner became a reality because of the tender mercy of God, who sent Jesus to illuminate the darkness of unbelief and to deliver sinners from the shadow of death. Jesus Himself is that Dayspring from on high, the Dawn, which brings light, dispels spiritual darkness, and causes the impending shadow of death to disappear. Moreover, He guides our feet in the way of peace, for, He, the Prince of Peace, brought peace on earth through His cross, so that St. Paul could say of Him, "He is our peace" (Eph. 2:14). This peace becomes the sinner's possession when he accepts Jesus as his Savior. "Therefore, being justified *by faith*, we have peace with God through our Lord Jesus Christ" (Rom. 5:1).

It should be noted that much of what the Holy Spirit says through the mouth of Zacharias is reminiscent of the prophetic writings which He spoke through the Prophet Isaiah, in particular:

Isaiah 9:2: "The people that walked in darkness have seen a great light; they that dwell in the land of the shadow of death, upon them hath the light shined."

Isaiah 60:1-3: "Arise, shine; for thy light is come and the glory of the Lord is risen upon thee. For, behold, darkness shall cover the earth, and gross darkness the people: but the Lord shall arise upon thee. And the Gentiles shall come to thy light, and kings to the brightness of thy rising."

The Benedictus *in the Worship of the Church*

The Benedictus is one of the three canticles taken from the New Testament which commemorate the incarnation of our Lord. The other two are *The Magnificat* and *The Nunc Dimittis*. Already in the middle of the fourth century these poetic Scriptures were appended to the Psalter and used as hymns of the ancient church.[9] In the medieval church, *The Benedictus* was appointed to be sung in the service of Laudes. Since the Reformation and the cessation of the canonical hours, *The Benedictus* has become an alternate choice of canticles for the worship at Matins. It is chanted usually on week days and on the Sundays in Advent and on the Sundays from Septuagesima to Palmarum.[10]

Chapter Notes

1. Cf. the naming of Jesus on the eighth day (Luke 2:21).
2. See Chase, Mary Ellen *The Psalms for the Common Reader*, New York, Norton Co., 1962, Part Two, "Their Poetic Structure," pp. 73-80.
3. *epeskepsato* = looked upon, to have care for.
4. *epoieesen lutroosin* = made redemption.
5. Some exegetes think that "horn" refers to horns fixed at the four

corners of an altar which persons seeking sanctuary could grasp. Arndt rightly considers the comparison of an animal's horn more natural. (See Arndt, William, *Bible Commentary, St. Luke*, St. Louis, Concordia, 1956, pp. 66, 67.)

6. Lenski writes at length about Zacharias's belief in verbal inspiration. See Lenski, R.C.H., *Interpretation of St. Luke*, Columbus, Lutheran Book Concern, 1934, sub. Luke 1:70.

7. "New Testament" refers to the new covenant in Christ's blood as compared to the covenant which shed the blood of goats and bullocks. (Cf. Heb. 9:11-28; I Pet. 1:18, 19.)

8. See Kretzmann, Paul E., *Popular Commentary*, St. Louis, Concordia, 1921, N.T., Vol. I, p. 268f., for quotations from Luther on *The Benedictus*.

9. Reed, Luther D., *The Lutheran Liturgy*, Philadelphia, Muhlenberg Press, 1947, p. 395.

10. Strodach, Paul Zeller, *A Manual on Worship*, Philadelphia, Muhlenberg Press, 1946 (revised edit.), p. 276.

FIVE

John the Baptist, Preacher of Repentance

All true Christian preachers are preachers of repentance, for the way into the kingdom of God is to repent and believe the Gospel. Great preachers of repentance before John the Baptist were: Noah, Moses, Elijah, and Jonah. Great preachers after John were: Peter, Paul, Augustine, Hus, and Luther. When John began his ministry, he cried: "Repent ye: for the kingdom of heaven is at hand" (Matt. 3:2). The One greater than John and all other preachers, whose way the Forerunner was sent to prepare, proclaimed the same message when He began His ministry (Matt. 4:17). Also, according to Luke 13:3 and 5, Jesus warned his hearers, "Except ye shall repent, ye shall all likewise perish." This statement enunciates the truth that without repentance there is no salvation.

Words Translated With "Repentance"

Two words from the Hebrew are translated "repent" in the *King James Version*. The first is *nacham,* which means literally "to sigh," "to breathe heavily." The other word of the Hebrew translated "repent" is *shub,* meaning "to turn back." *Shub* is also translated with the word "convert" in the *King James Version.*[1] *Metanoein* and its noun derivative *metanoia* are used 55 times in the New Testament. (*Metamelesthai* is used five times, and a derivative verbal adjective twice.) In the verses relative to John's preaching, only the verb *metanoein* and only the noun *metanoia* are used.[2]

"Repentance" Defined by the Scriptures

The Holy Scriptures, given by the inspiration of the Holy Spirit, interpret the Holy Scriptures. If one desires to know what "repentance" means, the answer is in the Scriptures. The Holy Spirit, the Author of the Bible, is its only competent interpreter.

Studying the Bible, we discover that the word "repent" is used in a restricted or narrower sense for "remorse," or what theologically is called "contrition." For example, Judas "repented himself" *(metameleetheis)*. He was filled with remorse that he had betrayed Jesus, but he did not trust in the Lord to forgive his sins. He despaired, hanged himself, and went "to his own place" (Acts 1:25). This restricted use of "repent" is apparent also in the following instances: In Jesus' invitation, "Repent ye and believe the gospel" (Mark 1:15), "repent" means to be sorry for one's sins. Similarly, when Jesus commanded that "Repentance and remission of sins should be preached in his name among all nations" (Luke 24:47), He referred to preaching the Law to work contrition, and preaching the Gospel to create faith in the forgiveness of sins. (See also Acts 20:21: "I . . . taught . . . testifying both to the Jews, and also to the Greeks, repentance toward God, and faith toward our Lord Jesus Christ.")

F. Pieper explains: "The term repentance *(metanoia)* is used in Scripture in a narrower and a wider sense (Trigl. 953, F.C. Sol. Decl., V,7). It designates a) contrition *(contritio)*, the knowledge of sin produced by the Law *(terrores conscientiae)*. Thus it is used in the passages where repentance is distinguished from the remission of sins, as in Luke 24:47: 'Repentance and remission of sins should be preached in His name among all nations.' It designates b) contrition and faith, or the entire conversion of man. Thus it is used Luke 15:7: 'Likewise joy shall be in heaven over one sinner that repenteth.' Heaven rejoices over the man who is saved, in whom there is contrition and faith. It is thus used also in Luke 13:3-5: 'Except ye repent, ye shall all likewise perish.' Used in the latter sense repentance is a synonym of conversion."[0]

The Formula of Concord (F.C.). alluded to by Pieper, declares: "The term repentance is not employed in the Holy Scriptures always in one and the same sense. For in some passages it is employed and taken for the entire conversion of man. . . But in Mark 1:15, as also elsewhere, where repentance and faith in Christ (Acts 20:21) or repentance and remission of sins (Luke 24:46, 47) are mentioned as distinct, to repent means nothing else than truly to acknowledge sins, to be heartily sorry for them, and to desist from them. This knowledge comes from the Law, but it is not sufficient for saving conversion to God if faith in Christ be not added, whose merits the comforting preaching of the Gospel offers to penitent sinners who are terrified by the preaching of the Law."[4]

When John the Baptist uses the word "repent," it means to change one's attitude toward sin and to trust in Christ for the remission of sin. (This changed attitude is also called "conversion" or "regeneration.") It is evident that repentance is a break with the past and a commitment to a new life in Christ. Thus St. Paul explains the fundamental transformation which occurs in a repentant sinner (2 Cor. 5:17): "If any man be in Christ he is a new creature: old things are passed away, behold all things are become new." (Comparing Paul's life before his conversion with his life after his conversion, we have a case history of what happens in the life of a sinner who has been turned to Christ.)

Repentance is a gift which God bestows. Acts 11:18 relates that the Jewish believers glorified God and gave Him credit for the conversion of the Gentiles: "When they heard these things, they held their peace, and glorified God, saying, Then hath God also to the Gentiles granted repentance unto life." Repentance (conversion, regeneration) is a miracle wrought by the Holy Ghost in the heart of natural man. Compare the passages of Scripture which speak of this transformation as a work of the Holy Spirit. Think especially of Titus 3:5: "Not by works of righteousness which we have done, but according to his mercy be saved us by the washing of regeneration, and *renewing of the Holy Ghost.*"

How John the Baptist Preached Repentance

The ministry of John the Baptist and the purpose of his preaching were described by his father Zacharias in prophecy as recorded in Luke 1:76-79: "And thou, child, shalt be called the prophet of the Highest: for thou shalt go before the face of the Lord to prepare his ways; to give knowledge of salvation unto his people by the remission of their sins, through the tender mercy of our God; whereby the dayspring from on high hath visited us, to give light to them that sit in darkness and in the shadow of death, to guide our feet into the way of peace." Mark alludes to the objective of John's preaching when he reports (1:4): "John did baptize in the wilderness, and preach the baptism of repentance *for the remission of sins.*" St. Paul's statement (Acts 19:4) also shows that John's purpose in preaching was to invite his hearers to accept Jesus as their Savior from sin: "John verily baptized with the baptism of repentance, saying unto the people, that they should believe on him which should come after him, that is, on Christ."

John proclaimed the Law to bring his hearers to the knowledge of their sins. He then proclaimed forgiveness through baptism. Examples of John's proclaiming of the Law to make sinners conscious of their sins are: "Then said he to the multitude that came forth to be baptized of him, O generation of vipers, who hath warned you to flee from the wrath to come" (Luke 3:7). "And now also the axe is laid unto the root of the trees; every tree therefore which bringeth not forth good fruit is hewn down and cast into the fire" (Luke 3:9). "He will throughly purge his floor, and will gather the wheat into his garner; but the chaff he will burn with fire unquenchable" (Luke 3:17).

By demanding "fruits meet for repentance,"[5] John the Forerunner led sinners to search their hearts and examine their lives. He counseled the people who asked, "What shall we do?" (Luke 3:10), by telling them, "He that hath two coats, let him impart to him that hath none; and he that hath meat, let him do likewise" (Luke 3:11). He told the publicans, Exact no more than that which is appointed you" (Luke 3:13). He gave soldiers who came to him a threefold directive: "Do violence to no man, neither accuse any falsely; and be content with your wages" (Luke 3:14).[6]

John, like all orthodox Christian preachers, was especially a herald of the Gospel.[7] The "baptism of repentance for the remission of sins" which John preached and invited sinners to receive is not explained, but it necessarily included the good news that God graciously forgives all sinners for the sake of the Lamb of God, and that this remission of sins is bestowed through baptism.

John the Baptist's most quoted, recorded statement of the Gospel is: "Behold the Lamb of God which taketh away the sin of the world" (John 1:29). After making this assertion, John identified Jesus as the eternal Son of God, made known to him when the Holy Spirit descended upon Jesus in the form of a dove at His baptism (John 1:30-34).[8]

The preaching of Law and Gospel is of the utmost importance today, as it was also in the ministry of John the Forerunner, because it pleased God by the foolishness of preaching to create faith (1 Cor. 1:21). After having convicted sinners of their sins by means of the Law, the Holy Spirit works godly sorrow (2 Cor. 7:10)[9] and faith in Jesus for the forgiveness of sins through the Gospel (Acts 20:21).[10]

29

Fruits Meet for Repentance

John the Baptist demanded "fruits meet for repentance" of the persons who came to be baptized. According to Acts 26:20, St. Paul also required works "meet for repentance:" "I . . . shewed first unto them of Damascus, and at Jerusalem, and throughout all the coasts of Judea, and then to the Gentiles, that they should repent and turn to God, and do works meet for repentance." Please note the order, "Repent and turn to God, and do works meet for repentance." But, did not John reverse this order: 1. Repent, 2. Turn to God, 3. Do works which prove that one is repentant? Did he not first demand "fruits meet for repentance" when the people presented themselves for baptism? It is true that he challenged "the multitude" (Luke 3:7, 8) and "many of the Pharisees and Sadducees" as to their sincerity when he saw them coming to be baptized, but there is nothing in the sacred record to suggest that he put persons on probation and refused to baptize them until they brought forth evident fruits of repentance. John preached that which Christian pastors teach today, that those who are sorry for their sins should resolve to amend their sinful lives. The Word of God also holds sinners who are repentant to make restitution when that is possible.[11]

What John the Baptist preached as a necessary part of repentance was sanctification. Repentance means, as a child once defined it, to be sorry enough to stop sinning. "Whosoever doeth not righteousness is not of God" (1 John 3:10). John was invoking the third use of the Law, that of a rule of life, when he told the publicans and soldiers and the people in general what they should do to prove their repentance.

There is nothing in the Four Gospels which suggests that John the Baptist made forgiveness (absolution) conditional. To make forgiveness conditional would vitiate the Doctrine of Objective Justification.[12] It would be saying to a person who has confessed his sins, "You must first prove that you are sorry for your sins before you can receive forgiveness for your sins." John, not being able to judge the heart as God can, accepted the confessions the people made as sincere, baptized the repentant sinners, and expected them thereafter to serve God with fruits of sanctification.

Chapter Notes

1. See Ps. 19:7; 51:13; Is. 6:10.
2. See Matt. 3:2; 3:8; 3:11; Mark 1:4; Luke 3:3; 3:8; Acts 19:4.
3. Pieper, Francis, *Christian Dogmatics,* St. Louis, Concordia, 1951,

Vol. II, p. 502.

4. Cf. Tappert, Theodore G., *The Book of Concord,* Philadelphia, Muhlenberg, 1959, p. 559.

5. *to de achuron katakausei puri asbestoo.*

6. It is interesting to note that Luke alone records the counseling of inquirers.

7. The very name "John" is Gospel, for it means "Jehovah is gracious."

8. Most exegetes regard John 1:16-18 as the comment of John the Evangelist. See Lenski, R.C.H., *The Interpretation of St. John's Gospel,* Columbus, Lutheran Book Concern, 1942, p. 87ff., for a discussion of reasons why these words should be regarded as written by the Evangelist under the inspiration of the Holy Spirit. The words of John 3:31-36, however, should be regarded as the words of the Forerunner.

9. 2 Cor. 7:10: "For godly sorrow worketh repentance to salvation not to be repented of: but the sorrow of the world worketh death."

10. See Walther, C.F.W., *The Proper Distinction Between Law and Gospel,* St. Louis, Concordia, transl. by W.T. Dau, 1928, Thesis XI, p. 236ff.

11. See Exodus 22:1-15; Luke 19:8; Eph. 4:28.

12. This cardinal doctrine of the Christian religion is the teaching that God has already forgiven all sinners for Christ's sake. See 2 Cor. 5:19-21; Rom. 5:18. The forgiveness which Christ has won for the world, and which God has declared as a judicial act, valid for all, is received through faith without any merit on the part of sinners. See Rom. 4:1-8.

S I X

The Baptism of John

The Gospels record a phenomenon in reporting the baptizing activity of John the Baptist. Although there were numerous uses of water for removing ceremonial defilement specified in the Law of Moses (Lev. 14:7, 27; 15:1-32; 16:26, 28; 17:15; Num. 8:7; 19:13; Deut. 23:10, 11), none of them is comparable to John's baptism of repentance for the remission of sins. His baptism was not repeated as were the Jewish baptisms of purification. And his baptism was not self-administered. It was a baptism for the forgiveness of sins and for salvation from the judgment of God.

If proselyte baptism[1] was in vogue among the Jews at the time of John, as Edersheim believes,[2] it was different from John's baptism in being self-administered; it was restricted to Gentiles who wished to embrace Judaism; it made the recipient ceremonially pure; but it did not place the proselyte into a reconciled relationship with God through the remission of sins. This was bestowed upon the believer through the sacrifices which were symbolic of the great sacrificial offering of the Messiah of which the Old Testament offerings were types and figures.

Although some scholars have precipitously reported affinity between John the Baptist and the Essenes, there are marked differences, not only in the general character of the movement, but in the sect's baptisms. Their lustrations were restricted to those persons who had made vows of holiness, they were repeated frequently, and they were of a ritualistic nature rather than a washing of forgiveness and renewal of the Holy Spirit.[3]

The Origin of John's Baptism

John's baptism was unique among baptisms and a phenomenon in this that he was known to his contemporaries as John the Baptizer. It is remarkably strange that John was not called the Way-preparer, the Forerunner, the Messenger, but was called John the Baptist by everyone, including Jesus.[4] Schlink declares: "If John's contemporaries had not regarded his Baptism as something new they would not have called John 'The Baptist' and would not have singled out his Baptism from the totality of his preaching and baptizing ministry as the decisive element."[5]

John himself provides the answer to the question about the origin of his baptism when he says in John 1:33: "I knew him not: but *he that sent me to baptize with water,* the same said unto me, Upon whom thou shalt see the Spirit descending, and remaining on him, the same is he which baptizeth with the Holy Ghost." Thus John's baptism had its origin with God. Also, Jesus implied that John's baptism was divine when He asked the chief priests, the scribes, and the elders: "The baptism of John, was it from heaven, or of men?" (Mark 11:30; Luke 20:4; cf. Matt. 21:25).

John's Baptism a Means of Grace

Isaiah's prophecy regarding the Forerunner spoke of his preaching as a message of comfort. The consolation consisted in the forgiveness of sins: "Cry unto her that her warfare is accomplished, that her iniquity is pardoned: for she hath received of the Lord's hand double for all her sins" (40:2).[6]

John himself said that the baptism which he was inviting the people to receive was "the baptism of repentance for the remission of sins" (Luke 3:3). John preached the Law with the purpose of showing his listeners their sins. When they confessed their sins, he baptized them to confer the forgiveness of sins: "Then went out to him Jerusalem, and all the region round about Jordan, And were baptized of him in Jordan confessing their sins" (Matt. 3:5, 6). But he refused to baptize the Pharisees and Sadducees who came to be baptized, demanding that they repent of their sins and bring forth fruits "meet for repentance," (the kind of conduct which would prove that they were sorry for their sins) (Matt. 3:7-12).

John the Baptist directed his hearers to the Savior who by His sacrifice would atone for the sins of the world. He told them, "Behold the Lamb of God which taketh away the sin of the world" (John 1:29). He identified Jesus, whom he had baptized, as the Son of God, attested by the voice of the Father and by the descent of the Holy Spirit. The baptism of repentance for the remission of sins was dependent upon the Redeemer to make it effectual for washing away sin.

Jesus' high regard for the baptism of John is revealed in His conversation with Nicodemus. Our Lord was referring to John's baptism when He told Nicodemus, "Except a man be born of *water and of the Spirit,* he cannot enter into the kingdom of God" (John 3:5). In this context Jesus spoke about the brazen serpent lifted up as a type of His crucifixion, and, in the treasured words of John 3:16, invited all sinners to be saved by believing in Him. In the course of His conversation with Nicodemus, Jesus explained that regeneration is necessary for a person to enter the kingdom of God because of man's sinful nature: "That which is born of the flesh is flesh; and that which is born of the Spirit is spirit" (John 3:6).

The fact that John's baptism was a means of grace, bestowing the forgiveness of sins, spiritual life, and eternal salvation is apparent also from the statements which Jesus made concerning the acceptance and the rejection of John's baptism: "And all the people that heard him, and the publicans, justified God, being baptized with the baptism of John. But the Pharisees and lawyers rejected the counsel of God against themselves, being not baptized of him" (Luke 7:29, 30). This means that the persons who believed, including the publicans, put their stamp of approval upon God's plan for saving sinners. On the other hand, the Pharisees and lawyers (scribes) nullified God's plan for their salvation by rejecting the baptism of John.

It should be noted that in the prophecy of Isaiah 40:5 the *Septuagint* translates the Hebrew *kepod yahweh* ("the glory of the Lord") with the Greek *to sooteerion tou Theou* ("the salvation of God"). The Holy Spirit interprets what the glory of the Lord is when St. Luke, following the *Septuagint,* writes: "And all flesh shall see the salvation of God" (3:6). This is a beautiful statement of God's universal grace offered through the baptism ministry of John the Forerunner of the world's Savior.

Baptism in the Early Church

The baptism of the apostolic church, like the baptism of John, was administered to the penitent: "Then Peter said unto them, *Repent,* and be baptized every one of you in the name of Jesus Christ for the remission of sins, and ye shall receive the gift of the Holy Ghost" (Acts 2:38). The baptism of the early church bestowed the forgiveness of sins: "Arise, and be baptized and wash away thy sins" (Acts 22:16). Christian baptism, like that of John, is a washing of regeneration and renewing of the Holy Ghost (Titus 3:5).[7] Both the baptism ordained by Jesus and that of John the Baptist bestowed the gift of salvation: "Baptism doth also now save us" (1 Pet. 3:21).[8] Galatians 3:26f. is applicable both to disciples of John and the disciples of Paul: "Ye are all the children of God by faith in Christ Jesus. For as many of you as have been baptized into Christ, have put on Christ." (Compare Acts 19:4: "Then said Paul, John verily baptized with the baptism of repentance, saying unto the people, that *they should believe on Him which should come after him, that is, on Christ Jesus.")*

We are convinced to conclude that the baptism of John and the baptism commanded by Jesus were essentially the same. The only difference is spelled out in Acts 19:4 (quoted above). John told the people to believe on the Savior *who was to come.* The baptism instituted by Jesus is administered with reference to the Savior *who has come,* suffered and died, arose from the dead, and ascended into heaven. It should be emphasized that there is only *one* baptism for the Church (Eph. 4:5).[9]

What About Acts 19:5?

Some Bible students have found difficulty with reference to John's baptism in Acts 19:5. These persons regard John's baptism as deficient, because of the statement: "When they heard this, they were baptized in the name of the Lord Jesus." If one regards these words as a continuation of Paul's narrative with reference to John the Baptist of verse 4, there is no difficulty. This is possible without violating the text. There are these considerations: 1. There is no indication in the New Testament that the disciples of John who became disciples of Jesus were rebaptized; 2. There is no indication that Apollos, *who knew only the baptism of John,* was baptized again (Acts 18:24f.); 3. The only reason these persons were deficient according to what the text says is that they had not received (not even heard about) the special gifts of the Holy Spirit bestowed upon the believers on Pentecost.[10]

Did John Practice Immersion?

Although it cannot be proved, it is commonly believed that immersion was the mode of baptism used by John the Baptist and by

Christians of the early church. Some persons, therefore, regard immersion as the only valid mode of baptism. The following are the chief reasons advanced for regarding immersion as the only acceptable way of baptizing: 1. The original meaning of the Greek verb *baptizein* is to dip, to immerse, to plunge under. Answer: The etymological meaning does not always prevail in the usage of a word. The contextual usage of the word determines what a word means in the New Testament. For example, *baptizein* plainly means "to wash" in Mark 7:4, Acts 22:16, Hebrews 9:10.[11] 2. John baptized in the Jordan River where there was sufficient water for immersion. It is expressly stated at a later time (John 3:23) that there was "much water" at Aenon where John was baptizing.[12] Answer: What about the instances when there was insufficient water for immersion? The statement regarding Aenon ("springs") refers to many *(polla)* springs or rivulets, and not to a large body of water. *The Didache* (second century) advises regarding the mode of baptism relative to circumstances:

"Concerning baptism, baptize in this way. Having first rehearsed all these things, baptize in the name of the Father and of the Son and of the Holy Ghost, in living [running] water. But if you have not living water, baptize into other water; and, if thou canst not in cold, in warm. If you have neither, pour water thrice on the head in the name, etc. . ."[13]

3. That immersion only gives the symbolism of a person buried with Christ by baptism to rise to newness of life. Answer: St. Paul in Romans 6:1-11 and in Colossians 2:8-14 speaks of the reality, namely, that Christians are partakers of Christ's death, burial, and resurrection. The symbolism of drowning the Old Adam by contrition and repentance is Martin Luther's application[14] of the reality which St. Paul affirms.

The Testimony of Archaeology

J.C. Davies has written relative to Romans 6:4 ("buried with him by baptism into death"):

"From this many writers have assumed that baptism was originally by total submersion, but the archaeological evidence all points to immersion with affusion as the normal practice. Examination of those frescoes in the catacombs which represent baptism and of the same scene on sarcophagi and engraved glass reveals no attempt to depict submersion; affusion is indeed shown, and the figures are usually naked, but the water only reaches to their ankles and there is no suggestion that the candidate plunges below the surface. It is moreover difficult to see how he could have done so in view of the shallowness of those fonts which have survived. The majority average from 2 to 4 feet in depth and any possibility of lying down is excluded by the insufficient diameter . . .

"The method employed for baptism, as the arrangement of the baptistry itself, was analagous to that of the public baths. In the frigidaria at Rome, the water was shallow and the bathers stood upright either in the flow from a projecting spout or pouring it over themselves. In the Lateran Baptistry Constantine placed on the rim of the font a golden lamb from whose mouth a stream of water gushed forth; the parallelism is obvious and leads to the conclusion that the officiant either guided the catechumen's head under the water or directed the flow on to his head with a vessel; this latter practice is evidence by the design on a spoon from Aquileia of the fourth or fifth centuries which shows a figure holding a *patera* in the stream of water over the head of the candidate. Where no fountain was provided the patera alone would suffice. It must however be admitted that the Pauline comparison of baptism with burial does suggest submersion, but the burial rites of the ancients were not the same as those in vogue today. When a body was laid to rest in the earth, the essential feature of the rite was the casting of a few handfuls of earth upon the corpse, hence the sprinkling of water on the candidate by affusion would appear to fulfill the essentials of comparison with burial. The archaeological evidence therefore strongly suggests the conclusion that submersion was not the original practice of the Church, but came to be thought the correct mode at a later age when infant baptism had become the prevalent custom [sic], and so by the ninth century submersion was commanded (Council of Chelsea, 816, canon 11)."[15]

The Symbolism of Water

The water used in baptism, although it is essential for the administration of the sacrament, is used symbolically for the cleansing from sin which occurs in baptism. The water itself does not cleanse from sin. It is "not the putting away of the filth of the flesh, but the answer of a good conscience toward God" (1 Peter 3:21). Luther aptly describes what occurs in baptism: "It is not the water indeed that does them, but the Word of God which is in and with the water. . ." This statement applies what Jesus told His disciples, "Now ye are clean through the word which I have spoken unto you" (John 15:3). Although water cannot be omitted in baptizing, it is irrelevant whether a small amount of water is used or whether the water is sufficient for immersion. It is beside the point to insist on immersing a person's entire body when the use of the water (though essential) is symbolic for the cleansing from sin by the Word of God.

Did John Baptize Infants?

There is no assertion in the Gospels or elsewhere in the Scriptures which reports that John the Baptist baptized or did not baptize little children. The same is true regarding baptism administered by the apostles in the early church. Nevertheless, it is credible that children were included in the households which are reported as receiving baptism: Cornelius (Acts 11:48); Lydia (16:15); the Jailer of Philippi (16:33). It is also believable that John baptized entire families, and that also infants were baptized. Parents were accustomed to bringing their male infants to the Lord by way of the Old Testament sacrament of circumcision. In Colossians 2:11f., Paul says that Christians are circumcised spiritually with the circumcision of Christ by being buried with Him in baptism. (The New Testament sacrament of baptism has replaced the Old Testament sacrament of circumcision.) In baptizing proselytes, a practice which seems to have been in vogue at the time of John, also the children of adults were baptized.

The reasons for the practice of infant baptism presented in compendiums of Christian doctrine are valid in considering the purpose of John's baptism: 1. Children are included in the "all nations" of the great commission of Matthew 18:28; 2. Baptism is the only means whereby infants (who, too, must be born again) can ordinarily be brought to faith (John 3:5f.; Gal. 3:26f.; Titus 3:5-7); 3. Because Jesus has declared that infants can believe in Him (Matt. 18:6) and can be subjects in His kingdom (Mark 10:13-15).

There is one passage of Scripture which usually is not considered relative to John's baptism ministry to children. That is the prophecy of Malachi regarding Elijah the prophet (identified by Jesus with John the Baptist in Matthew 17:12 and Mark 9:13): "He shall turn the heart of the fathers to the *the heart of the children* and *the children* to their fathers, lest I come and smite the earth with a curse" (Mal. 4:5). The Angel Gabriel referred to this prophecy when he told Zacharias (Luke

1:16f.): "And many of the children of Israel shall he turn to the Lord their God. And he shall go before him in the spirit and power of Elijah, to turn the hearts of the fathers to the children, and the disobedient to the wisdom of the just; to make ready a people prepared for the Lord." This means that John's ministry would have the spiritual objective of bringing young and old, children and adults, to faith in the promised Savior. In bringing the parents and their children to believe in Jesus, the "generation gap" would be removed, so that parents and children would have the same mind in Christ Jesus.

How did John endeavor to achieve this objective? By proclaiming the baptism of repentance for the remission of sins. John preached and baptized, but the Holy Spirit turned the hearts of parents and children; for repentance and faith are the achievements of the Holy Spirit of God. In the hearts of infants the Holy Spirit ordinarily works repentance and faith (as far as we know) only through the sacrament of baptism. On the basis of what the Bible says about the mission of John the Baptist, we may well conclude that he baptized also infants and brought them into the kingdom of God.

Precious Promises

The passage from Malachi and the words above in which reference is made to it by the Angel Gabriel comprise a precious promise which may be compared to the invitation of Simon Peter's Pentecost address: "Repent, and be baptized every one of you in the name of Jesus Christ for the remission of sins, and ye shall receive the gift of the Holy Ghost. For *the promise is unto you and to your children, and to all that are afar off, even as many as the Lord our God shall call*" (Acts 2:38f.). *Everyone present* was urged to repent and be baptized, for the promise was intended for young and old, parents and children.

The Blessings Wrought by John's Baptism

The baptism which John proclaimed and administered bestowed the blessing of the forgiveness of sins, reconciliation with God, the power for a new life of sanctification, and the certain hope of everlasting life to all those who received it, believing in the promised Savior.

Chapter Notes

1. Edersheim, Alfred, *The Life and Times of Jesus the Messiah,* Grand Rapids, Eerdmans, 1886, Vol. II, Appendix XII, pp. 745-747.

2. Op. cit., 747.

3. Lightfoot, J.B., *Saint Paul's Epistles to the Colossians and to Philemon,* Grand Rapids, Zondervan, 1976, p. 400.

4. Luke 7:28, 33.

5. Schlink, Edmund, *The Doctrine of Baptism,* St. Louis, Concordia, 1972, p. 19.

6. See our Chapter: *The Advent of John the Baptist in Prophecy.*

7. Cf. John 3:5.

8. Cf. Luke 7:29-30.

9. "One Lord, one faith, one baptism."

10. Acts 2:1-18. Cf. Acts 11:15-17.

11. Consider the wide range of meanings relative to water of the Greek verb *baptizein* in New Testament usage when Paul writes 1 Cor. 10:2: "baptized into Moses in the cloud and in the sea."

12. Lenski, R.C.H., *The Interpretation of St. John's Gospel,* Columbus, Lutheran Book Concern, 1942, p. 281.

13. Bettenson, Henry editor, *Documents of the Christian Church, New York & London, Oxford University Press, 1947,* "The Didache," p. 90.

14. "It signifies that the Old Adam in us should by daily contrition and repentance be drowned and die with all sins and evil lusts and, again, a new man daily come forth and arise, who shall live before God in righteousness and purity forever." (*Small Catechism,* The Significance of Baptism.)

15. Davies, J.G. *The Origin and Development of Early Christian Architecture,* New York, Philosophical Library, 1953, pp. 103-104.

SEVEN

Jesus Comes To Be Baptized

Jesus came from Galilee to Judea and the Jordan River to be baptized at the height of John's activity.[1] One of the purposes of John's baptizing ministry was for the Messiah to be manifested to Israel while John was engaged in this activity.[2] John had been informed (probably when the Word of God "came to him"): "Upon whom thou shalt see the Spirit descending, and remaining on him, the same is he which baptizeth with the Holy Ghost."[3]

Although John had been alerted that the promised Savior would be identified by the descent and continuing presence of the Holy Spirit, he evidently did not know that the Lord would *request* to be baptized. Therefore, when Jesus came to John to be baptized, the Forerunner said, "I have need to be baptized of thee, and comest thou to me?"[4] With these words John acknowledged: 1. His own need for baptism because he was a sinful human being, and confessed: 2. That Jesus did not need to be baptized because He was without sin. Jesus' answer to John's reluctance was, "Suffer it to be so now; for thus it becometh us to fulfill all righteousness."

It should be noted that our Lord includes both John and Himself in the words, "It becometh *us* to fulfill all righteousness." By baptizing Jesus, John would be doing God's will and would be furthering Jesus' mission to fulfill all righteousness. Although Jesus is the sinless Son of God, He presents Himself along with sinful human beings for baptism. Not that He needed the forgiveness which is offered, given, and certified by baptism, but by receiving the washing ordained for His brethren He put Himself in the same class as sinful human beings to keep the whole will and law of God in their stead. John's willingness to yield to Jesus' request to baptize Him proves his total devotion to do God's will.

The Mode of Jesus' Baptism

Despite the claims of some expositors that the words "went up straightway out of the water"[5] and "straightway coming up out of the water"[6] prove that Jesus was immersed, these words report only that Jesus stepped out of the water and stood on the bank of the Jordan River. The text does not say that Jesus was immersed. (The Greek word *baptizein* in New Testament usage has several connotations of applying water.)[7] It is not relevant whether Jesus was immersed or not. The command as it has been given to the Church means *to apply water* in the name of the Father and of the Son and of the Holy Ghost.

What Happened After Jesus Was Baptized?

In keeping with Luke's emphasis on prayer, his Gospel is the only one which reports that Jesus was praying after He stepped out of the water.[8] While He was praying, the heavens were opened.[9] Luther makes the comment: "When Christ became man and entered upon His preaching ministry, then heaven was opened. Beginning with that time, it is open and remains open. It has never again been closed since Christ's baptism in the Jordan; and it will never again be closed, hidden though this sight is from the physical eye."[10]

The words of the Father, "This is my beloved Son in whom I am well pleased," allude to Psalm 2:7: "Thou art my son, this day have I begotten thee," and Isaiah 42:1: "Behold my servant, whom I uphold; mine elect in whom my soul delightith." The voice from heaven can be identified because Jesus is called "My Son." Not only is there the phenomenon of the voice from heaven, but the Holy Spirit descended from heaven *in the form* of a dove and remained on Him. (How long the form of a dove was seen to remain, is not revealed; possibly long enough to indicate that the Spirit's gifts were bestowed upon Jesus permanently.)

Why the Holy Spirit appeared in the form of a dove is not explained in Scripture. Ylvisaker says: "The dove is in Scripture an emblem of peaceableness, meekness, simplicity (Cant. 1:15; 2:14; Hos. 7:11; Matt. 10:16). The point is not whether the dove is such a creature, but what it symbolizes in Scripture."[11]

The Son of God Made Manifest

John had been told by his Sender, "Upon whom thou shalt see the Spirit descending, and remaining on him, the same is he which baptizeth with the Holy Ghost."[12] What happened on the bank of the Jordan that day was an even greater manifestation for John the Baptist than had been promised. The heavens were opened, and the Father called down from heaven, "This is my beloved Son in whom I am well pleased." This Jesus, who was a relative of John, was identified by the Voice as the Son of God. The Forerunner told the effect that the Voice with the visual manifestation of the Holy Spirit had for him when he testified: "And I saw, and bare record that this is *the Son of God.*"[13]

The Holy Trinity Made Manifest

What occurred at the Jordan River after Jesus was baptized is a delineation of the doctrine of the Triune God. Here the Three Persons are manifested: The Son of God standing on the river bank, the Holy Spirit hovering above Jesus in the form of a dove, and the Father calling down from heaven with the testimony, "This is my beloved Son." Please compare this manifestation of the Holy Trinity with the command of Jesus' great commission to baptize all nations *in the name of the Father and of the Son and of the Holy Ghost.*[14] In Christian baptism a person is brought into a covenant with the Triune God who was manifested when Jesus was baptized.

Jesus' Anointing With the Holy Spirit

The Holy Spirit's descent upon Jesus at His baptism marked the beginning of His earthly ministry and office as our prophet, priest, and king. Not that Jesus was bereft of the Holy Spirit's presence with His human nature before the Spirit's descent occurred. He was conceived by the Holy Ghost! The visible descent of the Holy Spirit was a token of what had been bestowed at Jesus' incarnation. The anointing had been prophesied of the Messiah (the Christ) in Psalm 45.7 and Isaiah 61:1-3.[15] Peter in his address to the household of Cornelius (Acts 10:36-38) mentioned "the baptism which John preached" and declared: "God anointed Jesus of Nazareth with the Holy Ghost and with power." The prophets, priests, and kings in the Old Testament era were anointed with a measure of the Holy Spirit's gifts, but Jesus was anointed

43

without measure; He possessed all the gifts of the Holy Spirit for the administration of His threefold office.[16]

Did John Know Jesus?

In speaking about the baptism of Jesus and the manifestation of Jesus as the Son of God, John the Baptist said, "I knew him not: but that he should be made manifest to Israel, therefore am I come baptizing with water . . . And I knew him not: but he that sent me to baptize with water, the same said unto me, Upon whom thou shalt see the Spirit descending, and remaining on him, the same is he which baptizeth with the Holy Ghost. And I saw, and bare record that this is the Son of God" (John 1:31-34). John evidently was not speaking about personal acquaintance, for the Virgin Mary was related to Elisabeth, John's mother.[17] Although the home of Zacharias and Elisabeth, located somewhere in the hill country of Judea, was about eighty miles from Nazareth, where Jesus grew up, it is likely that John got to see Jesus during their boyhood years and beyond. (There were, for example, the feasts at Jerusalem which pious Jews attended faithfully.)[18] It is possible, of course, that an interval of years had intervened during which the physical appearance of Jesus would have changed considerably. But, John's protest that Jesus should rather baptize him than to be baptized by him leads one to believe that John knew Jesus personally and that he was speaking about the divinely assured certification needed to testify with certainty and assurance, "This is the Son of God."

Chapter Notes

1. "Now when all the people were baptized. . ." Luke 3:21. This activity according to John 1:28 occurred in *Bethabara* beyond Jordan. *Bethabara* is the reading in the *textus receptus*. A variant (adopted by recent translators) is *Bethany*. Neither of these places can be located in that region of the Jordan River. There is no good reason for rejecting the *Bethabara* reading.

2. John 1:31.

3. John 1:33b.

4. This conversation is recorded only in Matt. 3:14, 15.

5. Matt. 3:16a.

6. Mark 1:10.

7. See the previous chapter for a discussion of the meaning of *baptizein*.

8. Luke 3:21.

9. It is not mentioned in John's Gospel that the heavens were opened. This is recorded in all the Synoptic Gospels.

10. *Luther's Works,* Am. Edit., St. Louis, Concordia, 1957, Vol. XXII, p. 201.

11. Ylvisaker, John, *The Gospels,* Minneapolis, Augsburg, 1932, p. 119.

12. John 1:33.

13. Consider this manifestation relative to the question whether John's faith in Jesus was shaken during his imprisonment. See our Chapter: *Did John Doubt Jesus' Messiahship?*

14. Matt. 28:19.

15. Psalm 45:7: "Thou lovest righteousness, and hatest wickedness: therefore God, thy God, hath anointed thee with the oil of gladness above thy fellows."

Isaiah 61:1-3: The Spirit of the Lord God is upon me, because the Lord hath anointed me to preach good tidings unto the meek; he hath sent me to bind up the broken-hearted, to proclaim liberty to the captives, and the opening of the prison to them that are bound. To proclaim the acceptable year of the Lord, and the day of vengeance of our God; to comfort all that mourn; To anoint unto them that mourn in Zion, to give unto them beauty for ashes, the oil of joy for mourning, the garment of praise for the spirit of heaviness, that they might be called trees of righteousness, the planting of the Lord, that he might be glorified."

16. "Above thy fellows" (Psalm 45:7).

17. Luke 1:36.

18. Luke 2:41-44.

E I G H T

John the Baptist's Message

In Malachi 3:1a God promised to send His messenger. John the Baptist was that messenger. The Evangelist John writes (1:6): "There was a man sent from God whose name was John." The Forerunner spoke of his divine Sender in John 1:33: "And I knew him [Jesus] not: but he that sent me to baptize with water, the same said unto me, Upon whom thou shalt see the Spirit descending, and remaining on him, the same is he which baptizeth with the Holy Ghost." John also identified himself with the *voice* crying in the wilderness of Isaiah 40:3. John was sent to be "the prophet of the Highest," as Zacharias prophesied in *The Benedictus*. He was to be a spokesman for God, as the prophets who had preceded him. John was to be the last of the prophets; he would truly belong to the era of the Old Testament.[1]

The sacred historian Luke (3:1,2) defined precisely when John began his ministry as the spokesman for the Most High. He declared that "the word of God came unto John, the son of Zacharias, in the wilderness." This is the same way of expressing the commission of John as predicated of some of the Old Testament prophets.[2] This phrase denotes not only a divine call, but also the fact that God gave His spokesmen a revelation of what they were to say. Therefore, the words spoken by John the Baptist, like the words of the Old Testament seers, should be regarded as the inspired Word of the Holy Spirit.[3]

The Kingdom of Heaven and of God

The Gospel of Matthew reports (3:1,2): "In those days came John the Baptist, preaching in the wilderness of Judea,[4] and saying, Repent ye: for *the kingdom of heaven* is at hand." Similarly, Matthew writes that when Jesus began His public ministry in Galilee, after John had been imprisoned, He urged His hearers: "Repent for *the kingdom of heaven* is at hand."[5] The Evangelist Mark writes (1:14,15): "Now after that John was put in prison, Jesus came into Galilee, preaching the gospel of *the kingdom of God,* And saying: The time is fulfilled, and *the kingdom of God* is at hand: repent ye and believe the gospel." Also, when Jesus sent forth the Twelve on their mission tour, "He sent them forth to preach *the kingdom of God,* and to heal the sick."[6]

There is no difference between *the kingdom of heaven* and *the kingdom of God.* These are synonymous terms. The kingdom is not of this world, but has its origin with *the God of heaven.* Franzmann explains: "For John's contemporaries and countrymen 'heaven' was one of a number of reverential paraphrases for the name of God."[7] In the Gospel of Matthew, which was written chiefly for the Jews, the Holy Spirit, with a few exceptions, used the term "the kingdom of heaven."[8] In the other Gospels the expression "the kingdom of God" is used exclusively.

The Greek word which in the King James Version is translated "kingdom" is *basileia.* The basic meaning of *basileia* is "rule" or "reign."[9] Martin Luther, with his usual insight, answers the question of his *Small Catechism* (Second Petition of the Lord's Prayer) as to how the kingdom [rule] of God comes: "The kingdom of God comes to us when our heavenly Father gives us His Holy Spirit, so that by His grace we believe His holy Word and lead a godly life, here in time and hereafter in eternity."[10] Luther provides the following explanation in his *Large Catechism* (under the Second Petition):

"But what is the kingdom of God? Answer: Nothing else than what we learned in the Creed, that God sent His Son Jesus Christ, our Lord, into the world to redeem and deliver us from the power of the devil, and to bring us to Himself, and to govern us as the King of righteousness, life, and salvation against sin, death, and an evil conscience, for which end He has also bestowed His Holy Ghost, who is to bring these things home to us by His holy Word, and to illumine and strengthen us in the faith by His power."[11]

What Luther says about the meaning of "the kingdom of God is in agreement with the prophecy of Zacharias regarding John's message about the kingdom of God, that he would give "knowledge of salvation ... . by the remission of sins."[12] John preached entrance to the kingdom of God by proclaiming and offering the baptism of repentance for the remission of sins.

John preached with expectation and in anticipation of the kingdom: "The kingdom of heaven *is at hand*" (Matt. 3:2). And, he preached as the Forerunner of the Savior: "There cometh one mightier than I *after me*" (Mark 1:7).

John Proclaimed the Law

The Forerunner's preaching may be characterized as sin-conscious preaching. His intent was to prick the consciences of his hearers by revealing that there were aberrations in their lives. There were the "crooked" paths, which according to the prophecy of Isaiah, must be made straight, and the "rough places plain."[13] Sin is a reality which must be repented. John did not use kid gloves in dealing with sinners. He told the multitude, and the Pharisees and Sadducees in particular, that they were "a generation of vipers."[14] Which reminds us of Jesus' statement directed at the unbelieving Jews, "Ye are of your father the devil. . ."[15]

John pointed to individual sins when he answered the questions of the persons who asked what they should do to prove the sincerity of their repentance. He told the publicans that they should not exact a greater tax than was required. And he cautioned soldiers not to use violence, that they should not accused anyone falsely, and to be content with their wages.[16] The preachment of the Law which later resulted in John's martyrdom was his forthright condemnation of Herod's adultery and his censure "for all the evils which Herod had done."[17]

Besides exposing the sins of the persons in his audience, it was necessary for John to proclaim the punishment for sin and to warn against the righteous judgment of God upon transgressors. He spoke of "the wrath to come." He warned, "The axe is laid unto the roots of the trees: therefore every tree which bringeth not forth good fruit is hewn down and cast into the fire." He said of the mightier One: "He will baptize you . . . with fire: whose fan is in his hand, and he will throughly purge his floor . . . He will burn up the chaff with unquenchable fire."[18]

It was necessary for John to preach the Law in preparation for the Gospel, the message which soothes and comforts, after the Law has done its work of rousing consciences and terrifying sinners with the deserved judgment of a righteous God.

John Preached the Gospel

Zacharias, in *The Benedictus,* prophesied the gospel ministry of his son when he declared: "And thou child, shalt be called the prophet of the Highest: for thou shalt go before the face of the Lord to prepare his ways; *To give knowledge of salvation* unto his people *by the remission of their sins,* Through the tender mercy of our God; whereby the dayspring from on high hath visited us, To give light to them that sit in darkness and in the shadow of death, to guide our feet in the way of peace."[19]

John invited those who confessed their sins to receive baptism for the remission (forgiveness) of their sins. By assuring the people of the remission of sins, John bestowed the knowledge of God's salvation through Christ the Savior. The baptism of John, like the baptism authorized by Jesus in Matthew 28:19, was a means of grace and of eternal salvation.

John the Baptist not only proclaimed Jesus the Mightier One than he, who would baptize with the Holy Ghost, but pointed to Jesus as the Lamb of God "which taketh away the sin of the world." This concept compares the atoning sacrifice of our Lord to the sacrifices of the Old Testament which were offered as types of *God's* sacrifice on Calvary; Jesus is God's sacrificial offering. He took the sins of all mankind upon Himself and carried them away by atoning for them on the cross. The Apostle Peter writes: "Ye know that ye were not redeemed with corruptible things, as silver and gold, from your vain conversation received by tradition from your fathers; But with the precious blood of Christ, as of a *lamb* without blemish and without spot."[20] The Revelation of St. John, the Divine, speaks frequently of *the Lamb* and of *the blood of the Lamb.* In Rev. 7:14 the redeemed are described as "they who came out of great tribulation, and have washed their robes, and made them white *in the blood of the Lamb.*" Jesus is also identified with the pascal lamb in 1 Cor. 5:7: "Even Christ our passover is sacrificed for us." This adds to the concept of the forgiveness of sins the aspect of the deliverance from Satan and eternal death by Christ's death on the cross.

After John the Baptist identified Jesus as the Lamb of God, he declared that Jesus was revealed to him as the Son of God at His baptism.[21] Thus John proclaimed the same good news as St. Paul reported in 2 Corinthians 5:19: "God was in Christ, reconciling the *world* to himself, not imputing their trespasses unto them."

The quotations of John's message in the New Testament are a mere sampling of what he proclaimed in his preaching. This is evident from Luke 3:18: "And many other things in his exhortation preached he unto the people." A gospel statement which should be considered as the words spoken by John the Forerunner rather than the revelation given to John the Evangelist is recorded in John 3:31-36: "He that cometh from above is above all: he that is of the earth is earthly, and speaketh of the earth: he that cometh from heaven is above all. And what he hath seen and heard, that he testifieth; and no man receiveth his testimony. He that hath received his testimony hath set to his seal that God is true. For he whom God hath sent speaketh the words of God: For God giveth not the Spirit by measure unto him. The Father loveth the Son, and hath given all things into his hand. He that believeth on the Son hath everlasting life: and he that believeth not the Son shall not see life; but the wrath of God abideth on him."[22]

John the Baptist must have possessed a strong voice indeed to have reached the ears of the thousands who left the city of Jerusalem and the province of Judea and all the region near the Jordan River to hear him! John was, perhaps, the most naturally effective preacher of all the preachers mentioned in the New Testament: as persuasive as Peter, as fervent as Paul, as eloquent as Apollos. The excerpts of John's preaching in the Gospels are only samples which give the flavor and substance of what he said.[23]

No better summary of the content of John's message and its purpose can be recorded than the four verses of John 1:6-9: "There was a man sent from God, whose name was John. The same came for a witness of the Light, that all men through him might believe. He was not that Light, but was sent to bear witness of that Light. That was the true Light which lighteth every man that cometh into the world."[24] These verses also indicate that the Gospel predominated in the preaching of the Forerunner. The proclamation of the Law was a preliminary necessity to prepare the hearts of sinners for his real message, the Gospel.[25]

Chapter Notes

1. Jesus declared (Luke 7:28) that there was no greater prophet than John the Baptist, and added, "But he that is least in the kingdom of God is greater than he." Our Lord evidently was referring to believers of the New Testament era.

2. See Jer. 1:1-5; Ezek. 1:3; Hosea 1:1,2; Joel 1:1; Jonah 1:1; Micah 1:1; Zeph. 1:1; Hag. 1:1; Zech. 1:1.

3. John was filled with the Holy Spirit from his mother's womb (Luke 1:15c, 41, 44).

4. The Judean wilderness was bounded on the west by the plateau, and on the east by the Dead Sea and the southern part of the Jordan River.

5. See Matt. 4:17.

6. Luke 9:2.

7. Franzmann, Martin H., *Follow Me: Discipleship According to Saint Matthew,* Saint Louis, Concordia, 1961, p. 16.

8. Exceptions are: 6:33; 12:28; 19:24; 21:31; 21:43.

9. *Basileia* has numerous connotations. Sometimes it is used in the sense of "realm," and is used to denote the whole number of believers. See *Bible Key Words,* a translation of Gerhard Kittel's *Theologisches Woerterbuch Zum Neuen Testament,* Vol. II, New York, Harper, 1958, III *Basileia.*

10. Luther, Martin, *A Short Explanation of Dr. Martin Luther's Small Catechism,* St. Louis. Concordia, 1943, p. 155.

11. Tappert, Theodore G., transl., & ed., *The Book of Concord,* Philadelphia, Muhlenberg Press, 1959, p. 426f.

12. Luke 1:77.

13. Is. 40:4.

14. Matt. 3:7; Luke 3:7.

15. John 8:44a.

16. Luke 3:12-14.

17. Luke 3:19.

18. Matt. 3:10-12. Cf. Luke 3:7-9, 16.

19. Luke 1:76-79.

20. 1 Peter 1:18,19.

21. John 1:30-34.

22. The King James Version does not differentiate between words spoken (quoted) and the statements of the sacred writers. More recent translations which use quotation marks indicate whether the translators considered the words of John 3:31-36 as the words of John the Baptist or not. Recent translations which indicate that John spoke these words are: *The New Testament in Modern English* (Phillips), *The New International Version,* and *God's Word.*

23. Edersheim, Alfred, *Life and Times of Jesus the Messiah,* Grand Rapids, Eerdmans, 1886, Vol. 1, p. 337 refers to Kelm's observation that

John, thoroughly acquainted with the Book of Isaiah, derived many of his picturesque metaphors from the Old Testament prophet.

24. John 1:9 is better translated: "The true Light which enlightens everyone was coming into the world." Jesus said of Himself (John 8:12): "I am the light of the world: he that followeth me shall not walk in darkness, but shall have the light of life."

25. See Walther, C.F.W, *The Proper Distinction Between Law and Gospel,* St. Louis, Concordia, 1928.

N I N E

John the Baptist
and the Essenes

The Gospels have numerous references to the Pharisees and Sadducees, religious sects among the Jews. Also, frequent mention is made of the Samaritans, a people who had a mixture of heathen elements in their religion. There is also recognition in the New Testament of the presence of a patriotic party among the Jews called the Zealots[1]

But, there is no mention of the religious sect of the Essenes. If this seems strange, it is surprising also that there is no reference to the Essenes in the *Talmud*. That such a sect existed at the time of Jesus and of John the Baptist is reported by Philo, the Jewish philosopher from Alexandria (30 B.C.- 50 A.D.), by Josephus Flaxius, the Jewish historian (37-100 A.D.), and Pliny the Elder, a Roman historian (23-79 A.D.).

The Dead Sea Scrolls

In 1947 the first Dead Sea Scrolls were discovered in the region of the Dead Sea, and subsequently (beginning in 1952), excavations of Khirbet Qumran on the northwest corner of the Dead Sea revived interest in the Essenes, because most scholars identified the ascetic community with the sect described by Philo, Josephus, and Pliny.[2] Archaeological research has determined that the site was occupied by an ascetic community 110 B.C. to 31 B.C. and reoccupied by the same sect 4 B.C. to 68 A.D. Scholars studying the Dead Sea Scrolls have noted much information about the beliefs and practices of these people in addition to what Josephus, Philo, and Pliny reported about the Essenes.

The Roots of Essenism

The origin of the Essenes as a religious sect among the Jews is obscure. It is believed that a party zealous for the observance of the Ceremonial Law, known as the *Chasidim* or *Hasidaioi* (the pious), arose sometime before the Maccabaean wars. Both Pharisaism and Essenism seem to have had their roots in the *Chasidim* movement toward a studied piety. According to the judgment of Lightfoot,[3] ceremonial purity was an absorbing passion of the Essenes, that is, they were more zealous (sincere) than the sect of the Pharisees in the pursuit of a strict mode of life. As for the etymology of the name Essene—it is unknown.

The Influence of the Essenes?

In the nineteenth century, Joseph Ernest Renan put forth the idea that the Christian religion had its origin in Essenism. Renan, and others after him, insisted that the Essenes influenced both Jesus and John the Baptist. Coincidental and superficial similarities were exaggerated, and differences were disregarded or minimized.

After the discovery of the Dead Sea Scrolls and the excavation of Khirbet Qumran on the northwest shore of the Dead Sea, speculation that John the Baptist was a member of the Essene sect was renewed. The thinking of those scholars who identified John as an Essene followed this line of reasoning: 1. Since St. Luke reports that Zacharias and Elisabeth were advanced in years when John was born, it is possible that he was adopted by the sect and brought up in their beliefs and customs.[4] 2. It has been said that John's austere life-style reflects the ascetic practices of the Essenes. 3. The fact that John was "in the deserts till the day of his shewing to Israel"[5] and that the Word of God came to John "in the wilderness"[6] has been offered as evidence that he was a member of an Essene desert community. 4. Also, the baptism which John proclaimed and administered has been likened to the ceremonial lustrations of the Essenes.

What Can Be Asserted With Certainty?

More recently, scholars have pointed out the essential facts of John's background and the differences which should be noted relative to the teachings and observances of the Essenes.

First, and above all, it should be emphasized that John the Baptist was born into the home of parents who "were righteous before God, walking in all the commandments and ordinances of the Lord blameless."[7] His father was a priest of the Most High, and his mother was of the daughters of Aaron, the first high priest called by God to offer sacrifices and to intercede for His people. Zacharias was an orthodox priest in the midst of a corrupt church, a church split into factions. The predominant sect was the Pharisees. But, many of the priests of that time belonged to the select, smaller sect of the Sadducees.[8] They denied the possibility of miracles, the immortality of the soul, the resurrection of the body, and the existence of angels. There is no evidence that Zacharias was either a Pharisee or a Sadducee. His son, John the Baptist, denounced both the Pharisees and Sadducees as a "generation of vipers."[9]

John the Baptist, no doubt, knew of the Essenes and had contact with them,[10] for it is evident from his preaching and from his counsel to the publicans and to the soldiers who asked, "What shall we do?"— that he knew what was happening in the world about him.[11] Why didn't John denounce the Essenes as he did the Pharisees and Sadducees? Evidently because he did not have occasion to do so. (It is likely that at least one of the Gospel writers would have reported the confrontation.) The Essenes probably did not come to him, but remained aloof because of the very nature of their separatistic way of life.

All that is revealed about John the Baptist in the Gospels bespeaks his unique personality and delineates his singular office. John would be described today as "a loner." There are both minor and major differences distinguishing him from the Essenes:" 1. John wore a garment woven of camel's hair like his prototype, the Prophet Elijah. The Essenes of the Qumran community donned white ceremonial robes. 2. John's preaching of repentance and his message regarding the kingdom of God has no parallel in the scrolls.[12] 3. Although the Essenes offered gifts to be used for the Temple, they did not believe in nor participate in the sacrifices. John, however, was alluding to the symbolism of the sacrifices of the Temple when he pointed to Jesus as the Lamb of God who takes away the sin of the world.[13] 4. The baptism of John was for the remission of sins, and was administered once as a means of grace for entrance to the kingdom of God. The lustrations of the Essenes occurred daily and had the purpose of making them a ceremonially pure people of God. 5. John's invitation to receive the kingdom of God was extended to all sinners. The Essenes considered themselves a select people of God. 6. John the Baptist was filled with the Holy Spirit from his mother's womb and called by God for the special ministry of the Savior's forerunner. The Essenes did not have an unction of the Holy Spirit, and were not called by God to their way of life. 7. The Word of God came to John the Baptist, that is, his teachings were given to him by direct revelation of the Holy Spirit, as they were revealed to the Old Testament prophets. Although the Essenes had the Scriptures and valued them. Their understanding of them was corrupted by their self-conceived teachings and customs.

What has so far been revealed by the Dead Sea Scrolls, regarding the Essenes[14] substantiates that the Christian religion is unique and had its origin with God, as contrasted with the religious teachings and the ritual of Qumran.

John the Baptist was God's prophet, and more than a prophet, for he was sent to prepare the way of the Lord. His was a unique mission and ministry. His message came from God, and was not derived from the teachings of the Essenes.

Chapter Notes

1. See Luke 6:15 and Acts 1:13.

2. Pliny declares that the Essenes lived "on the west side away from the shores" of the Dead Sea. (*Historica Naturalis,* 5:17). See Pfeiffer, Charles, *The Dead Sea Scrolls and the Bible,* Grand Rapids, Baker, 1969, Weathervane edition, New York, no date, p. 96.

3. Lightfoot, J.B., *St. Paul's Epistle to the Colossians and to Philemon,* a Revised Text, Grand Rapids, Zondervan, 1959, p. 356.

4. According to Josephus, *Antiquities* XIII, V, 9, the Essenes did not marry. But there is evidence at Qumran that some of the sect married. (See Pfeiffer, op. cit., p. 138.)

5. Luke 1:80.

6. Luke 3:2.

7. Luke 1:6.

8. This has been inferred from Acts 5:17. Josephus (*Antiquities* XX, 9, 1) says that Annas, the high priest, was a member of the Sadducees.

9. Matt. 3:7.

10. Otto Betz has expressed the view that John the Baptist was raised in the Qumran community, that he was influenced by their teachings, but that he left to preach to a wider audience of Jews. See Shanks, Hershel, ed., *Understanding the Dead Sea Scrolls,* New York,

Random House, 1992, p. 206.

11. Luke 3:12-14.

12. Graystone, Geoffrey, *The Dead Sea Scrolls and the Originality of Christ,* New York, Sheed and Ward, 1956, p. 95.

13. John 1:29.

14. Scholars charged with editing the remaining scrolls have been dilatory in completing publication, so that the contents of the remaining scrolls is not generally known.

TEN

In the Spirit and Power of Elias

The last prophecy of the Old Testament is recorded in the last two verses of the last chapter of Malachi. The Lord says through the pen of the prophet (Malachi 4:5, 6): "Behold, I will send you Elijah the prophet before the great and dreadful day of the Lord: And he shall turn the heart of the fathers to the children, and the hearts of the children to their fathers, lest I come and smite the earth with a curse."

The Expectation That Elijah Would Come

The Pharisees who came from Jerusalem to interrogate John knew the prophecy of Malachi, for they asked John, "Art thou Elias?" Evidently they believed that Elijah would come in the flesh.

It appears that there was a rather general expectation that Elijah would return.[1] When Jesus and His disciples came into the region of Caesarea Philippi, He asked them, "Whom do men say that I the Son of Man am?" One of the answers He received was *Elias* (Matt. 16:14; Luke 9:19). Herod also was told by those around him that some people believed that Elijah had appeared (Mark 6:15; Luke 9:8). It seems from the context of some of these expressions that the belief of those who spoke of Elijah's coming was that he would rise from the dead and return to a prophetic ministry on earth. This is not the same as a belief in reincarnation.[2]

Jesus Identifies John as the Elijah of Malachi

After the transfiguration, when Peter, James, and John asked Jesus, "Why say the scribes that Elias must first come?" (Mark 9:11; cf. Matt. 17:10), Jesus answered (Matt. 17:11,12); "Elias truly shall first come, and restore all things. But I say unto you, That Elias is come already, and they knew him not, but have done to him whatsoever they listed. Likewise shall also the Son of Man suffer of them." Thus Jesus Himself declared that the prophecy of Malachi was fulfilled by the coming and ministry of John the Baptist. Matthew explains that the disciples understood that Jesus was speaking of John the Baptist.

How Was John Like Elijah?

There are quite a number of similarities in the careers of John the Baptist and Elijah: 1. Both lived in a time of great spiritual recession; 2. Both received direct revelations from God; 3. Both lived lives of austerity; 4. Both wore a garment of animal hair;[3] 5. Both reproved the ruler in power; 6. Both were objects of a queen's wrath.

There are differences: 1. John did no miracles; 2. John's distinctive mission was to baptize for the remission of sins; 3. Elijah was translated to heaven without experiencing death—John died a martyr's death.

In what way was Elijah a prototype of John the Baptist? The answer to this question is in the prophecy of Gabriel, spoken when he announced the birth of the Forerunner to his father in the Temple, Luke 1:17: "And he shall go before him in the spirit and power of Elias to turn the hearts of the fathers to the children, and the disobedient to the wisdom of the just; to make ready a people prepared for the Lord."[4] The Holy Spirit empowered and made the preaching and baptism of John effectual.

John may have had the gift of the Spirit to work miracles as Elijah had done, but he did not use it.[5] John's gifts of the Holy Spirit were manifested in the conversions which occurred when he preached the Gospel and baptized those who came to him.[6] Through his Spirit-blessed ministry the hearts of children and adults were turned to the wisdom of justified (forgiven) sinners. Thus John the Forerunner fulfilled his mission of preparing the hearts of many people for the indwelling of the Lord. John's success in accomplishing his mission was not due to personal magnetism, nor because of the exceptional talents he had, but to the Holy Spirit's endowment.

59

Chapter Notes

1. Evidently, the prophecy of Malachi was generally known and believed.

2. Reincarnation is the belief that a deceased person will live again in *another* body. This is not the same as the Biblical doctrine of the resurrection of the (same) body in a glorified state.

3. 2 Kings 1:8.

4. Gabriel's words are interpretive, and they are an application of Malachi's prophecy. The prophecy declares that the differences between the children and adults will be resolved, and that the curse (upon sinners) will be revoked.

5. Did John have the Spirit-given power to work miracles? The question cannot be answered. (In the early church not all Christians possessed the same gifts of the Spirit. See 1 Cor. 12:4-11). If John had the gift of miracles, he desisted from using it. His call did not include miracle-working.

6. Elijah's great miracle on Mt. Carmel resulted in the return of many in Israel to the Lord. The conversions resulting from John's ministry are comparable to the results of Elijah's great victory on Carmel. Elijah and John were motivated by, and their mission was empowered by the same Holy Spirit.

ELEVEN

John the Baptist's Disciples

Some of John's disciples became Jesus' disciples. The Fourth Gospel reports that the Forerunner directed Andrew and another disciple, who was probably John the Evangelist, to Jesus, "the Lamb of God which taketh away the sin of the world." They spent the rest of that notable day with Jesus and became His disciples. Subsequently, also Simon Peter and Nathanael became the Savior's followers. It may be that some of the other eight disciples were also previously disciples of the Baptist.

Not a few Bible scholars have supposed that there was a rift between John's remaining disciples and Jesus. These scholars have found the seed for this opinion in John 3:25f. There the evangelist reports that the Forerunner's disciples came with what might be viewed as a complaint against Jesus. That is, they said that the Person of whom John had borne witness beyond Jordan was baptizing, and all men were coming to Him.

What John Answered About Jesus

The news which John's disciples brought evoked an explanation from him: "A man can receive nothing, except it be given him from heaven." He reminded his disciples, "Ye yourselves bear me witness, that I said, I am not the Christ, but that I am sent before him."

John described himself as the friend of the Bridegroom who rejoices "because of the bridegroom's voice." Then he added, "He must increase, but I must decrease."

The Forerunner also proclaimed Jesus as the One above all who came down from heaven. He spoke of Jesus as having been anointed with the Holy Spirit above measure. He concluded with what is recorded in verse 36: "He that believeth on the Son hath everlasting life: and he that believeth not the Son shall not see life; but the wrath of God abideth on him."

If John's disciples were in any way at odds with Jesus or His disciples, it surely was not encouraged by John's witness about Jesus. One may believe that John's disciples accepted John's glowing testimony and believed in Jesus as their Lord and Savior, although they still considered John their mentor and continued as his loyal disciples as long as he was alive.

A Question About Fasting

An instance of John's disciples questioning the teaching and practice of Jesus is recorded in Matthew 9:14-17. They confronted Jesus with the question, "Why do we and the Pharisees fast off, but thy disciples fast not?" (Mark 2:18 and Luke 5:33 reveal that the Pharisees were present when the question was asked.) The question of John's followers was prompted, as Lenski comments, not by hostility, but by perplexity.[1]

Jesus' answer did not command nor forbid fasting, but He told John's disciples by illustrations that it was incongruous for His disciples to fast while He was still with them.[2]

John the Baptist had already been imprisoned by Herod Antipas at this time when his disciples asked Jesus the question about fasting. They still regarded John as their master. But, it should be noted that they did not hesitate to ask Jesus about a matter which disturbed them.

John's Disciples Report Jesus' Miracles

Although John was in prison, his disciples had visitation rights. Thus Luke reports (7:18) that his disciples, who probably did not have firsthand information about Jesus' activity, visited John in prison and told him about the miracles which everyone was discussing (17). Evidently these disciples were loyal to John and had not yet joined themselves with Jesus' disciples to accompany Him. There is no evidence that they were unfriendly or antagonistic toward Jesus. John sent them to Him, so that they might have firsthand knowledge of His miracles and to ask Him the important question, "Art thou he that should come? Or do we look for another?"[3]

John's Disciples Tell Jesus

How sorrowful John's disciples were when they found out about their master's manner of death! They claimed the headless body and gave it honorable burial. Then they went to tell Jesus.

The Gospels of Matthew and Mark, which alone tell about the gruesome circumstances of John's death, do not reveal what comfort Jesus gave the grieving disciples. But, the very fact that they went to Jesus to tell Him the sad news shows that they were disposed to confide in Him.[4]

Disciples of John at Ephesus

The ministry of John the Baptist had wider results than just the conversions in Judea and in the region near the Jordan River. Some persons who repented of their sins and received John's baptism later traveled to other regions throughout the Roman Empire. Thus the Gospel was brought to Alexandria, Egypt. It was there that Apollos, a Jew, brilliant and eloquent, and well-versed in the Old Testament (the *Septuagent*), came to Ephesus and spoke in the synagogues about the imminent coming of the Messiah. Apollos had received instruction about the kingdom of God, and had been baptized; but he had not heard about Jesus' advent, death, resurrection, and ascension. Priscilla and Aquilla, who had remained in Ephesus after Paul had gone to Jerusalem (to keep a vow), heard Apollos preach, and took him aside to tell him about Jesus whose way John had prepared. After this necessary briefing, Apollos was disposed to go to Corinth, so the Christians at Ephesus wrote to the disciples there, urging them to receive him.[5]

Paul returned to Ephesus sometime after Apollos went away to Corinth. Here the apostle found twelve men, believers in Christ, who had not heard about the outpouring of the gifts of the Holy Spirit on Pentecost. These men, like Apollos, had been baptized with the baptism of John. (It seems that they did not have any connection with Apollos's ministry in Ephesus.) It appears that they were more informed than Apollos had been before Priscilla and Aquilla instructed him. It is clear that Paul did not find it necessary to instruct them as Priscilla and Aquilla had instructed Apollos.

Some Bible readers believe that the baptism of these men was deficient, that they did not know the Triune God. They understand the statement of Acts 19:5 as if it referred to what Paul *did*. But verse 5 may be taken as a continuation of what Paul *said* about the witness of John and the baptism which followed the Forerunner's witness about the Lord Jesus: "When they heard this [John's invitation to believe in Jesus] they were baptized in the name of the Lord Jesus." (This was the view of the eminent theologian, Martin Chemnitz.)[6]

The isolated instances of John the Baptist's influence do not prove that there was a separate "Baptist Movement" as some scholars contend. The very examples of Apollos and of the twelve believers who entered the mainstream of the early church exclude any notion that the New Testament supports the theory that communions of John the Baptist's disciples existed separate and apart from the Christian churches.[7]

Chapter Notes

1. Lenski, R.C.H., *Interpretation of St. Matthew's Gospel,* Columbus, Wartburg Press, 1943, p. 367.

2. Matt. 9:15-17.

3. See our Chapter: *Did John Doubt Jesus' Messiahship?*

4. Matt. 14:12.

5. Acts 18:27.

6. See Pieper, Francis, *Christian Dogmatics,* St. Louis, Concordia, 1953, Vol. III, p. 288; Koehler, E.W.A., *Summary of Christian Doctrine,* River Forest, IL., Koehler Publishing Co., 1939, p. 184, (altered in revised edit., 1952, by Alford W. Koehler, p. 202).

7. *Recognition of Clement,* Chapter 54, *The Ante-Nicene Fathers* ed. by A. Roberts and J. Donaldson, New York, The Christian Literature Co., 1890, p. 92, links later followers of John the Baptist with Simon Magus. Evidently this is a fabrication originating with persons hostile to the Forerunner, for Simon Magus is characterized as an arch-heretic.

TWELVE

Did John Doubt
Jesus' Messiahship?

The ministry of the Forerunner was less than a year and a half in duration.[1] It was interrupted when Herod Antipas imprisoned him because he reproved the king for having taken his brother Philip's[2] wife and for other public sins. According to Josephus, John was imprisoned in Machaerus, a mountain fortress east of the Dead Sea.[3]

John was allowed to have visitors in prison, so that his disciples could come to see him. They came to him with the news that Jesus was doing many miracles. The narrative gives the impression that John's disciples did not have personal knowledge of these miracles, but that the rumor of what was happening in Galilee had become the subject of conversation in Judea.[4] When John learned of what Matthew calls "the works of Christ," he sent two disciples to ask Jesus the question, "Art thou he that should come, or do we look for another?" (Matt. 11:3; cf. Luke 7:21).

Most expositors have misunderstood the reason why John sent disciples to Jesus with the question. They surmise that John became despondent in his imprisonment because Jesus was not bringing judgment upon the wicked. Some expositors go so far as to say that John's faith failed.[5] Other commentators, more conservative, declare that John had doubts of a temporary nature, and that his faith was bolstered by the report which his disciples brought back to the prison.[6]

The Mission of John's Disciples

Matthew's reference to John's hearing about "the works of *Christ*" suggests that John, who was thoroughly acquainted with the prophecies of Isaiah, recognized the miracles as those which Messiah (the Christ) would perform. That is, John sent his disciples to Jesus, so that they would be convinced by Jesus personally of His divine Messiaship.

It is notable that John sent *two* disciples to Jesus. Two is the number demanded for valid testimony[7]. These two disciples were, according to Luke 7:21, witnesses of what the Lord did while they were present: "And in that same hour he cured many of their infirmities and plagues, and of evil spirits; and unto many that were blind he gave sight." Then Jesus told them: "Go your way, and tell John what things ye have seen and heard; how that the blind see, the lame walk, the lepers are cleansed, the deaf hear, the dead are raised, to the poor the gospel is preached." These divine works correspond to those which were prophesied of the Messiah in the book of Isaiah.[8]

Jesus deferred to John as the teacher of the two disciples when He told them to tell John the things they had seen and heard. But He added for the particular benefit of the disciples, "And blessed is he, whosoever shall not be offended in me" (Matt. 11:6; Luke 7:23). This beatitude urges John's disciples to put aside any doubts that He is the promised Christ.[9]

It is not at all in keeping with the character of John the Baptist, who was filled with the Holy Spirit from his mother's womb, who had received the special sign of the Holy Spirit descending upon Jesus at His baptism, who had testified so eloquently about the Son of God and the Lamb of God who takes away the sin of the world—that he would come to doubt Jesus' messiahship and confess his doubtful state of mind by sending disciples to bring back assurance for himself! Surely, the Forerunner, who had been equipped with the gift of the Holy Spirit[10] for his unique office, would not yield to doubt because he was suffering imprisonment for Christ![11] Consider further whether Jesus could have delivered the ecomium for John which followed after He sent the disciples back to report to John. A discussion of these positive characterizations follows:

Jesus' Glowing Commendation

After John's disciples departed, Jesus spoke with approbation regarding the character and conduct of John. He did this mostly in the form of questions: "What went ye out into the wilderness to see? A reed shaken with the wind?" (John's character was resolute, not vacillating.) "But what went ye out for to see? A man clothed in soft raiment? Behold, they that wear soft clothing are in king's houses." (John could have lived in luxury at the court of Herod, but he had chosen to reprove the king and to be imprisoned. He wore a garment of camel's hair, the austere trademark of a prophet coming in the spirit and power of Elijah.) "But what went ye out for to see? A prophet? Yea, I say unto you, and more than a prophet. For this is he, of whom it is written, Behold I send my messenger before thy face, which shall prepare thy way before thee." (Jesus extolls the office of His Forerunner as being more than that of a prophet. His mission was singular, one that no servant of God had ever held.) "Verily I say unto you, Among them that are born of women there hath not risen a greater than John the Baptist . . ." (Jesus affirms with authority that John is the greatest human being ever born, because of his unique office.) But then Jesus adds: "Notwithstanding, he that is least in the kingdom of heaven is greater than he." (Why is the lowliest person in the kingdom of heaven greater than John the Baptist? Because that person is privileged to view what Jesus did for our salvation as an accomplished fact. John could view Jesus' mission only from the perspective of one who believed that the prophecies would be fulfilled.)

Surely, all that Jesus said regarding John supports the explanation that John sent his disciples to Jesus to give *them* the assurance that He is the promised Messiah.

Opposition and Rejection

"And from the days of John the Baptist until now the kingdom of heaven suffereth violence, and the violent take it by force." (Some expositors take this double statement to refer to the large influx of converts which began during the ministry of John. But, it would be strange to think of the kingdom of heaven *"suffering* violence" by sinners coming to believe, and of violent persons exorting force to enter the kingdom of heaven. Rather, this verse speaks of persons like the scribes and Pharisees who were trying to enter the kingdom of heaven by work righteousness. They are the kind of persons who do not enter by the Door (John 10:1-9).[12]

John the Baptist was the terminus for prophecy. He was/is the last prophet before the great and dreadful day of the Lord. A new era began with his unique ministry. Jesus declared that John the Baptist is the Elias (Elijah) whose coming was promised by Malachi (4:6).

Finally, Jesus compared the way in which His contemporaries reacted to the ministry of Jesus and of John to children playing in the market place. Some want to play "wedding," but others do not want to play a game which requires happy expressions. But, when it is suggested that they play "funeral," they are not agreeable! Thus the people of that generation expressed their unhappiness with John the Baptist when he came abstaining from rich food and strong drink.[13] They said that he was possessed with a devil.[14] Jesus came exercising a different life-style; He ate and drank and socialized with all classes. They said that He was a gluttonous man, a wino, and a friend of publicans and sinners.

"But wisdom is justified of her children." (The wisdom of the Gospel is vindicated by those who receive it into believing hearts.)[15]

"But the Pharisees and lawyers rejected the counsel of God against themselves, being not baptized of him." (The members of the Pharisee sect and the scribes rejected God's plan of salvation by rejecting John's baptism.)[16]

Chapter Notes

1. John began his ministry in the Spring of 26 A.D. It came to an end in the Summer of 27 when Herod imprisoned him.

2. Philip, the husband of Herodias, was a half brother of Herod Antipas.

3. Josephus, Ant. XVIII, 5, 2.

4. According to Luke 7:11-17, Jesus had raised the young man of Nain. The effect of this miracle is stated in verses 16 and 17: "And there came a fear on all: and they glorified God, saying, That a great prophet is risen among us; and, That God hath visited his people. And this rumor of him went forth throughout all Judea, and throughout all the region around about." John's disciples told him about this report circulating in Judea.

5. Stalker, James, *The Two Johns of the New Testament,* London, Isbister and Company Limited, 1895, p. 244, entitles Chapter 4: "The Eclipse of His Faith."

6. For the various interpretations of John's sending his disciples to Jesus, see Ylvisaker, John, *The Gospels,* Minneapolis, Augsburg, 1932, pp. 302-304.

7. They were to serve as witnesses, and two was the minimum

number necessary for establishing what is true. Cf. Num. 35:30; Deut. 17:6; 19:15; Matt. 18:16; 2 Cor. 13:1; 1 Tim. 5:19.

8. Isaiah 35:5, 6: "Then the eyes of the blind shall be opened, and the ears of the deaf unstopped. Then shall the lame man leap as an hart, and the tongue of the dumb sing: for in the wilderness shall waters break out, and streams in the desert."

Isaiah 61:1: "The Spirit of the Lord God is upon me; because the Lord hath anointed me to preach good tidings unto the meek. . ."

9. Martin Luther: "It is certain that John proposes the question for the sake of his disciples, for they did not yet deem Christ to be He whom they should believe Him to be. And John had not come to draw disciples and the people to himself, but to prepare the way for Christ and bring all men to Christ, making them subject to Him . . . But when Jesus began to perform miracles and was widely spoken of, then John thought he would dismiss his disciples from him and bring them to Christ, in order that they might not after his death organize a hereditary [sic] sect and become Johannites, but all cling to Christ and become Christians; and he sent them that they might learn, not henceforth from his testimony, that He was the right man of whom John had spoken." (Quoted by Kretzmann, Paul E., *Popular Commentary,* St. Louis, Concordia, 1921, N.T., Vol. I, p. 61.)

10. Kretzmann writes: "John himself, filled with the Holy Ghost from his birth, having been a witness of the revelation of God and being thoroughly convinced of Christ's Messiahship, Luke 3:15; John 1, 15. 26. 33; 3, 28, had no doubts concerning Christ and His mission." (op. cit., p. 61).

11. See Sieck, Henry, *Sermons on the Gospels of the Ecclesiastical Year,* St. Louis, Concordia, 1906, for an excellent sermon on Matt. 11:2-10 (the Standard Pericope for the Third Sunday in Advent), p. 14ff.

12. Some exegetes refer to Luke 16:16, "And every man presseth into it," as if it could be used to give Matt. 11:12 the meaning that many persons were being converted. But Arndt, William F., *Bible Commentary the Gospel According to St. Luke,* St. Louis, Concordia, 1956, p. 361, explains: "'Everybody tries to press into it.' *Biazetai* is best taken in the conative sense and as a middle. The proclamation of the coming of the kingdom created excitement, and everybody desired to get the benefit of its divine sway and blessings. However, the gate to the kingdom, if we conceive of it as a city, is narrow. One must repent to enter, and many try to rush into the region of bliss without passing through that gate. They think they can force their way into it, taking

along all filthy *impedimenta,* their favorite sins, their evil associations and habits. As a result great numbers have to remain outside."

13. John's food was locusts and wild honey (Matt. 3:4c; Mark 1:6c). As a Nazarite he did not drink wine or liquor.

14. Jesus here reveals that John was the object of his generation's hatred, even as Jesus was hated and misrepresented.

15. Faith is an assertion that the Gospel is true. Cf. John 1:33: "He that hath received his testimony hath set to his seal that God is true."

16. Many of the Pharisees and Sadducees came desiring baptism (Matt. 3:7-12). But they refused to repent and believe the Gospel. Jesus declared that the Pharisees and lawyers (scribes) rejected God's plan for their salvation by refusing baptism. Please note that Jesus regarded (and recommended) the baptism of John as a means of grace and salvation.

THIRTEEN

The Imprisonment, Death, and Burial of John

John the Baptist began his ministry in 26 A.D. He had been preaching and baptizing less than a year and a half when he was imprisoned by Herod Antipas. He had endured the imprisonment for about two years when he was murdered.

Strangely, the circumstances of John's incarceration and death are reported only by Matthew and Mark,[1] and then because of Herod's superstition that the wondrous works which Jesus and His disciples were doing—were being wrought by John the Baptist risen from the dead. The Gospel of Mark provides the most detailed account of how it came about that John was imprisoned and how he suffered a martyr's death.[2]

John's Imprisonment

The Gospels do not reveal the occasion or circumstances of John's accusation that Herod was living in an adulterous marriage. Evidently John spoke out fearlessly and in such a way that the accusation confronted Herod: "It is not lawful for thee to have thy brother's wife" (Mark 6:18). This accusation angered Herod and infuriated his adulterous spouse. At the time the incident occurred, Herod was angry enough to condemn John to death, but he feared the effect this would have on the people of his realm because they regarded the fearless preacher as a prophet (Matt. 14:5). Herodias was determined that John must die, but Herod opposed this and imprisoned him and thus "kept him safe" (Mark 6:17-20). According to Josephus, John was imprisoned in Machaerus, a fortress constructed by Herod the Great.[3] There the Tetrarch had occasion to summon John and listen to his teachings. Although he was disturbed by what the righteous preacher said, he enjoyed listening to him.[4] Herod's later sorrow indicates that he not only admired John, but had even grown to like him.[5]

But, Herodias was intolerant of what John had said about her unlawful marriage and waited for a "convenient day" for revenge. That day came when Herod threw a lavish party on his birthday for his nobles, military commanders,[6] and foremost men of Galilee.

Herodias Grasps Her Opportunity

Salome, the daughter of Herodias by her former (legal) marriage, provided entertainment for Herod's guests at his birthday party by dancing for them. The sacred narrative does not tell what kind of dance it was. It may have been an erotic performance, as has been suggested by playwrights[7] who have embellished the mere mention provided in the Gospels. That the dance pleased Herod so much that he promised his "stepdaughter" anything she desired up to half of his kingdom indicates that her performance was unusual.

It is unlikely that Herodias schemed with an ultimate purpose to have her daughter dance at Herod's party, although she may have done so. But, when Herod promised Salome anything she would ask for, Herodias seized the opportunity. Salome went to her mother and naively said, "What shall I ask for?" The reply came, apparently without hesitation, "Ask for the head of John the Baptist." No time intervened, Salome returned to Herod immediately and said: I will that thou give me by and by[8] [at once] in a charger [platter] the head of John the Baptist." (Whether the platter was Salome's or Herodias's idea cannot be determined.)

It is likely that Herod made his reckless promise under the influence of wine, but then realized what a rash thing he had done. He was truly sorrowful to kill the courageous preacher, but because of his oath and to save face before his guests,[9] he ordered a guard to bring him the head of John the Baptist. The guard emerged momentarily with the gory head of the godly prophet on a platter. He gave the grewsome gift to the girl, and she carried it to her mother.

The Entombment

When John's disciples heard about his decapitation, they claimed his body and laid it in a tomb. It is doubtful that these remains included the head delivered to Herodias. It is unlikely that she would have given it to his devout disciples for honorable burial.

The Gospels do not reveal the site of John's tomb. Tradition gives the location of his grave as Nablus, which is the ancient Sichem, a town of Samaria. Jerome (+420 A.D.) refers to John's sepulchre at Sebaste,[10] one of the cities rebuilt in Samaria by Herod the Great.[11] A tradition of unlikely verity is that the body of the martyr was transferred to Alexandria, where a church was erected to honor him in the fourth century.[12]

The Cathedral of Aachen, West Germany, claims possession of a linen cloth "in which the head of John the Baptist was wrapped after decapitation."[13] There is a tradition that John's head has been preserved in a marble sarcophagus in a chapel of the Ommayyad mosque at Damascus.[14] If this does not satisfy the credulity of the gullible, there is the legend that his head was brought to Constantinople in the fourth century under Emperor Theodosius, and that a fragment of it was reputed to have been brought to the Cathedral of Amiens in the thirteenth century.[15]

Chapter Notes

1. Matt. 14:1-12; Mark 6:14-29.

2. *Martyr* (deriv. Greek) originally referred to a witness. It came to have the connotation of a witness who was slain because he confessed his faith in Jesus. Bible readers usually think of Stephen (Acts 7) as the first martyr. John the Baptist was actually the first witness slain for his faithful stance as a spokesman for Christ. It was part of his testimony to condemn sin to prepare his hearers for the Gospel.

3. Josephus, *Antiquities,* Book XVIII, V, 2.

4. Mark 6:20.

5. Matt. 14:9; Mark 6:26.

6. *Chillarchois.*

7. Krummacher, Friedrich Adolph, *Johannes,* Stuttgart, Harre, 1818. Sudermann, Hermann, *John the Baptist,* transl. by Beatrice Marshall, London & New York, John Lane Co., 1909. Wilde, Oscar, *Salome,* transl. from the French by Lord Alfred Douglas, New York, Heritage Press, 1945.

8. *Exautees.*

9. Note that two reasons are given (Mark 6:26) why Herod did not reject Salome's request.

10. Emminghaus, Johannis H., *St. John the Baptist (the Saints in Legend and Art)* Rechlinghausen, Aurel Bongers, 1967, p. 12.

11. Josephus, *Antiquities,* Book XV, VIII, 5.

12. Horn, Edward T., III, *The Christian Year,* Philadelphia, Muhlenberg Press, 1957, p. 195.

13. Air France Travel Blurb, *Sanctuaries and Pilgrimages,* printed in France, imprimeries Paul Dupont, no date.

14. Baum, Peter (pseudo.), Emrich, *Early Sites of Christianity,* New York, Pantheon, 1957, pp. 176-179.

15. Sicre, Raymond, *Amiens Cathedral,* Ouest-France, 1990, p. 3. Bergeaud, Jean, *Saint John the Baptist,* (transl. by Jane Wynne Saull, New York, Macmillan, 1962, pp. 65 & 67, reports that the relic was proven in 1958 to be spurious.

FOURTEEN

Regard for John Outside Christendom

The Mandaeans

The name Mandaeans means "those who know," and is derived from "manda," (Syriac—"mad'a") which means as much as divine knowledge. The Mandaeans are an ancient sect similar to the Gnostics of the 2nd and 3rd centuries. Their origin is obscure, possibly Babylonian, judging from mythological elements. Their religion is a strange mixture of pagan, Jewish, and Christian features. There are about 2,000 Mandaeans today in lower Mesopotamia (Iraq).[1]

In the seventeenth century Christian missionaries, mistaking their ablutions and their high regard for John the Baptist as evidences of Christianity, called the Mandaeans "St. John's Christians."[2] But, strangely, the Mandaeans's deference to John grew out of their hostility to the Christian religion.

The Mandaean sacred books, written in an Aramaic dialect of Babylon (7th & 8th centuries A.D). are: 1. *The Ginza,* or *Treasure;* 2. *The John Book;* 3. *The Qolasta* (a kind of hymn book). *The John Book* contains a legendary version of John's birth of Zacharias and Erishbai (Elisabeth). The passages referring to John are infrequent and lack details.[3] The account of Jesus' baptism is hostile toward Him, for it says that He would "pervert the Baptism of Jordan, distort the words of truth, and preach fraud and malice" in all the world.[4]

The passages relating to John the Baptist in the Mandaean sacred books belong to the most recent writings or appear as obvious interpolations. No historical link between the original disciples of John and the Mandaeans can be established.[5]

Islam

John the Baptist is regarded in the Mohammedan religion as one of the greatest prophets. The *Koran* refers to the annunciation to Zacharias in detail in the following two passages:

"There Zacharias called on his Lord, and said, Lord, give me from thee a good offspring, for thou art the hearer of prayer. And the angels called to him, while he stood praying in the chamber, saying, Verily God promiseth thee a son named John, who shall bear witness to the Word which cometh from God, an honorable person, chaste, and one of the righteous prophets. He answered, Lord, how shall I have a son, when old age hath overtaken me, and my wife is barren? The angel said, So God doth that which he pleaseth. Zacharias answered, Lord, give me a sign. The angel said, Thy sign shall be, that thou shalt speak unto no man for three days, otherwise than by gestures, remember thy Lord often, and praise him evening and morning."[6]

"A commemoration of the mercy of thy Lord toward his servant, Zacharias. When he called upon his Lord, invoking him in secret, and said, O Lord, verily my bones are weakened, and my head is become white with hoariness, and I have never been unsuccessful in my prayers to thee, O Lord. But now I fear my nephews, who are to succeed after me, for my wife is barren: wherefore, give me a successor of my own body from before thee; who may be my heir, and may be an heir of the family of Jacob; and grant, O Lord, that he may be acceptable unto thee. And the angel answered him, O Zacharias, verily we bring thee tidings of a son whose name shall be John; we have not caused any to bear the same name before him. Zacharias said, Lord, how shall I have a son, seeing my wife is barren, and I am now arrived at a great age, and am decrepit? The angel said, So shall it be: thy Lord saith, This is easy for me; since I created thee heretofore, when thou wast nothing. Zacharias answered, O Lord, give me a sign. The angel replied, Thy sign shall be that thou shalt not speak to men for three nights, although thou be in perfect health. And he went forth unto his people, from the chamber, and made signs unto them, as if he should say, Praise ye God in the morning and in the evening. And we said unto his son, O John, receive the book of the law, with a resolution to study and observe it. And we bestowed on him wisdom, when he was yet a child, and mercy from us, and purity of life, and he was a devout person, and dutiful towards his parents, and was not proud or rebellious. Peace be on him the day whereon he was born, and the day whereon he shall die, and the day whereon he shall be raised to life."[7]

It is interesting to note that the *Koran* in the main does not differ greatly from the Gospel of Luke. Yet there are significant difference in details, as for example, the length of the period of silence imposed upon Zacharias, three days as compared to nine months. Also, apparently, the silence pertained only to speaking to men. Strangely, the name John is represented as being unknown among the Jews, whereas the persons present at the circumcision of the child said there was no relative who bore the name John. The last lines quoted above from the *Koran* purport to be a blessing spoken upon the child John by angels.[8]

The Mormons

The person of John the Baptist looms large in the religion of the Church of Jesus Christ of Latter Day Saints. This is brought to the attention of visitors to Temple Square in Salt Lake City, the church's headquarters. There within the enclosure is a bronze and granite monument depicting John the Baptist's conferring the Aaronic priesthood upon Joseph Smith and Oliver Cowdery. The statues, sculptured by Avard Fierbanks, are 1 1/4 life-size, and show Smith and Cowdery kneeling, while John the Baptist, standing, has his right hand on the head of the Prophet and his left hand on the head of Cowdery. A similar monument has been erected near Harmony, Pennsylvania, on the banks of the Susquehanna River, where it is alleged the priesthood was conferred. This incident, which a Mormon writer calls "one of the world's great events,"[9] is described by Joseph Smith as occurring on May 15, 1829, as follows:

"We still continued the work of translation, when in the ensuing month (May, 1829), we on a certain day went into the woods to pray and inquire of the Lord respecting baptism for the remission of sins, that we found mentioned in the translation of the plates. While we were thus employed, praying and calling upon the Lord, a messenger from heaven descended in a cloud of light, and having laid his hands upon us, he ordained us, saying: Upon you my fellow servants, in the name of Messiah, I confer the Priesthood of Aaron, which holds the keys of the ministering of angels and of the gospel of repentance, and of baptism by immersion for the remission of sins; and this shall never be taken again from the earth until the sons of Levi do offer again an offering unto the Lord in righteousness.

"He said this Aaronic Priesthood had not the power of laying on hands for the gift of the Holy Ghost, but that this should be conferred on us hereafter; and he commanded us to go and be baptized, and gave us directions that I should baptize Oliver Cowdery, and that afterwards he should baptize me.

"Accordingly we went and were baptized. I baptized him first, and afterwards he baptized me—after which I laid my hands upon his head and ordained him to the Aaronic Priesthood, and afterwards he laid his hands on me and ordained me to the same Priesthood—for so we were commanded.

"The messenger who visited us on this occasion and conferred this Priesthood upon us, said that his name was John, the same that is called John the Baptist in the New Testament, and that he acted under the direction of Peter, James, and John, who held the keys of the Priesthood of Melchizedek, which Priesthood, he said, would in due time be conferred on us, and that I should be called the first Elder of the Church, and he (Oliver Cowdery) the second. It was on the fifteenth day of May, 1829, that we were ordained under the hand of this messenger, and baptized."[10]

John the Baptist is not mentioned by name in the *Book of Mormon,* but numerous passages pertaining to him are revised and enlarged in Joseph Smith's Version of the Bible. Also, John the Baptist was a frequent topic in the sermons and writings of Joseph Smith.[11]

Chapter Notes

1. *Encyclopedia Britannica,* Chicago, 1981, sub. Mandaeans.
2. *Encyclopedia Britannica,* op. cit.
3. Steinmann, Jean, *Saint John the Baptist and the Desert*

Tradition, transl. from the French by Michael Boyes, New York, Harper Brothers, 1958, p. 130.

4. Steinmann op. cit., quoting Thomas' *Le mouvement baptiste en Syrie et en Palestine* (p. 258), p. 129.

5. Steinmann, op.cit., p. 131.

6. *The Koran,* translated from the original Arabic by George Sale, 8th edit., Philadelphia, Lippincott, 1913, Chap. III, p. 40.

7. *The Koran,* op. cit., Chap. XIX, pp. 248-249.

8. *The Koran,* op. cit., Chap. XIX, p. 249.

9. Barton, Peggy, *John the Baptist,* Salt Lake City, Deseret, 1978, p. 109.

10. Smith, Joseph, *Doctrine and Covenants & the Pearl of Great Price,* Salt Lake City, Church of Jesus Christ of Latter Day Saints, 1949, *Pearl of Great Price,* Part 2, #68-72.

11. Barton, op. cit., p. 110.

**Monument in Temple Square
Salt Lake City, Utah**

FIFTEEN

John the Baptist
a Pattern for Preachers

Jesus spoke with reference to John the Baptist's unique office as His forerunner when He declared: "Among them that are born of women there hath not risen a greater than John the Baptist" (Matt. 11:11). John was a prophet, for he spoke for the Most high. But he was more than a prophet because he was the messenger sent to prepare the way of the Lord (Matt. 11:9, 10). He was commissioned to go before Jesus in the spirit and power of Elijah to turn the hearts of the people of Israel to the Lord their God (Luke 1:16,17). According to the prophecy of the Angel Gabriel, John was to be great in the sight of the Lord.

The manner in which John the Baptist discharged his great office received the singular commendation of the Lord when He spoke of John's ministry and told the unbelieving Jews: "He was a burning and a shining light [lamp]"[1] (John 5:35). No greater tribute has ever been given a messenger of the Gospel than this testimony of the Son of God. This estimate of John recommends the study of his character and career, so that pastors today may follow his example. The Holy Spirit did not discard the mold when He made John the Baptist "a burning and a shining light." The Lord's ambassadors today by His grace can also yield themselves to His will to serve faithfully for His eternal glory.

John's Call
The son of Zacharias and Elisabeth was destined from eternity to

be the Way-preparer of the Messiah, Jesus Christ. The Holy Spirit prophesied his mission through His Prophets Isaiah and Malachi. And, when the fullness of the time for the incarnation of the Son of God drew near, the Angel Gabriel appeared to Zacharias as he was offering incense in the Temple at Jerusalem and announced the miracle-birth of a son whose name was to be John. This child was to be filled with the Holy Spirit from his mother's womb. The remarkable circumstances of John's birth would cause the people of the hill country of Judea to exclaim, "What manner of child shall this be!"

John received the Old Testament sacrament of circumcision on the eighth day after he was born. The thirty years following are summarized in Luke 1:80: "And the child grew, and waxed strong in spirit, and was in the deserts till the day of his showing unto Israel." This is the only information which the Bible provides regarding John's childhood, youth, and growth to manhood.[2]

The call to begin his ministry of preaching and baptizing came to John the Baptist in the wilderness when he was thirty years old. Luke 3:1f. gives the following data: "Now in the fifteenth year of the reign of Tiberius Caesar, Pontius Pilate being governor of Judea, and Herod being tetrarch of Galilee, and his brother Phillip tetrarch of Iturea and of the region of Trachonitis, and Lysanias the tetrarch of Abilene, Annas and Caiaphas being the high priests, the word of God came unto John the son of Zacharias in the wilderness." This terse statement, "The word of God came unto John," indicates that John had a divine call to preach the Word of God to Israel. John himself speaks of that call when he refers to the One who sent him to baptize with water.[3]

John accepted his divine commission and "came into all the country about Jordan, preaching the baptism of repentance for the remission of sins" (Luke 3:3). Similarly, preachers today will answer the call to proclaim the Gospel which the Lord extends to them, though the call is not issued directly, but through a Christian congregation.[4]

John's Self-Denial

John the Baptist was chosen by God to be a Nazarite, that is, a person set apart to serve Him in a special way.[5] Accordingly, the Angel Gabriel announced to his father Zacharias: "He shall be great in the sight of the Lord, and shall drink neither wine nor strong drink; and he shall be filled with the Holy Ghost even from his mother's womb" (Luke 1:15). That John strictly observed the vow of the Nazarite is evident from Jesus' statement, "John came neither eating or drinking, and they say, He hath a devil" (Matt. 11:18; cf. Luke 7:33).

John's life was marked by austerity also in this that his food was locusts and wild honey; and his raiment was woven of camel's hair. Locusts, permitted for food by Leviticus 11:22, were the food of the very poor;[6] and the rough garment of camel's hair was the trademark of the prophets.[7] John's lifestyle was one of self-denial.

Although John's abstinence and austere manner of life do not commend themselves to our Western culture, his self-denial is worthy of emulation. Ministers, too, are tempted to be Gentile-minded (worldly) in asking, "What shall we eat? or What shall we drink? or Wherewithal shall we be clothed?" (Matt. 6:31). Some ministers are too much occupied with the quality of food and drink, the cut of their clothes, and the comfort of their living conditions. But, self-indulgence does not nurture spiritual life, not contribute toward building the kingdom of God. It is relevant for ministers to be mindful of the Scriptural exhortation. "Endure hardness as a good soldier of Jesus Christ" (2 Tim. 2:3). Above all, ministers of Jesus Christ should remember His directive for discipleship: "If any man will come after me, let him deny himself, and take up his cross, and follow me. For whosoever will save his life shall lose it; and whosoever will lose his life for my sake shall find it" (Matt. 16:24f.).

John's Humility

John knew and was mindful of the vast difference between himself and the eternal Son of God made flesh. Moreover, he identified Jesus as the pre-existent Lord when he told his hearers: "This was he of whom I spake, He that cometh after me is prefered before me: for he was before me" (John 1:15). John also revealed a humble spirit under his Lord when he said: "I indeed baptize you with water unto repentance: but he that cometh after me is mightier than I, whose shoes I am not worthy to bear: he shall baptize you with the Holy Ghost, and with fire" (Matt. 3:11). The baptism with the Holy Ghost occurred on Pentecost.[8]

Matthew quotes John as saying that he is not worthy to bear Jesus' shoes. Mark, Luke, and John quote the Forerunner's statement that he is unworthy to loose the latchet of Jesus' shoes. This seeming discrepancy is explained by the consideration that John stated his regard for Jesus in somewhat different words as he was preaching day after day.[9]

John the Baptist also revealed his humble character when Jesus

82

came to him to be baptized: "I have need to be baptized of thee, and comest thou to me?" (Matt. 3:14).

Pastors, more than other Christians, should remember that the Lord Jesus answered the question, "Who is greatest in the kingdom of heaven?" by calling a little child and setting him in the midst of the disciples. He said: "Verily I say unto you, Except ye be converted, and become as little children, ye shall not enter into the kingdom of heaven. Whosoever therefore shall humble himself as this little child, the same is greatest in the kingdom of heaven" (Matt. 18:3, 4). More than John the Baptist, Jesus has given us an example of humility. In the night in which He was betrayed, He girded himself with a towel, took a basin, and washed His disciples' feet. Afterwards, He said to them: "Know ye what I have done to you? Ye call me Master and Lord: and ye say well; for so I am. If I then, your Lord and Master, have washed your feet; ye also ought to wash one another's feet. For I have given you an example, that ye should do as I have done to you" (John 13:12c-15). Our Lord also exhorted: "Take my yoke upon you, and learn of me; for I am meek and lowly in heart; and ye shall find rest for your souls" (Matt. 11:29). It is truly a beautiful metaphor which the Holy Spirit employs when Peter urges Christians to be "clothed with humility" (1 Pet. 5:5). No more appropriate vestment can be worn by a servant of the Lord and minister of the Gospel than a cloak of humility.

John's Self-efacement

The spirit of humility is evinced also in John's self-negation. When his disciples came to him with the complaint that the One to whom he had borne witness beyond Jordan was baptizing, and all men were coming to Him, John answered: "A man can receive nothing except it be given him from heaven. Ye yourselves bear me witness, that I said, I am not the Christ, but that I am sent before him. He that hath the bride is the bridegroom: but the friend of the bridegroom, which standeth and heareth him, rejoiceth greatly because of the bridegroom's voice: this my joy therefore is fulfilled. He must increase, but I must decrease" (John 3:27-30).

Instead of being filled with envy, John rejoiced at the large following of Jesus. He had no inflated notions about his own importance, nor did he have aspirations for future glory or recognition. John accepted his declining status and the growing reputation of his Lord as a fulfillment of his joy.

John's words, "He must increase, but I must decrease," are a recommendable motto for ministers of the Gospel. They spell out total dedication for the work of the Lord's kingdom. Similarly, Paul the apostle was concerned only that Christ would be magnified in his body, whether by his life or by his death.[10] What John and Paul are telling ministers of the Word today is, "to God alone be the glory."

John's Piety

There is no indication in the New Testament as to how many childhood years John the Baptist had the blessing of parental guidance. Zacharias and Elisabeth were both well stricken in years at the time of their son's birth. If they lived long enough for the young child to observe their godly conduct, he had a good example for his own life, for Luke writes that Zacharias and Elisabeth walked "in all the commandments of the Lord blameless" (Luke 1:6).

Whether John had the memory of godly parents or not, he grew up to live an examplary life. Mark 6:20 states that "Herod feared John, knowing that he was a just man and an holy."[11] Evidently, the fruits of faith were manifest in John's life, so that Herod regarded him as a godly person, feared him, and resisted Herodias's efforts to harm him.[12]

Not only preaching the commandments as a guide for sanctification is necessary in the life of a Christian pastor, but an accompanying virtuous life. Pastors are to be "ensamples" (examples) to the flock (1 Pet. 5:3). They must be able to say as Paul exhorts (Phil. 3:17): "Brethren, be followers together of me, and mark them which walk so as ye have us for an example." Moreover, Paul urges the young minister, Timothy, to exercise himself "unto godliness," and adds, "For bodily exercise profiteth little: but godliness is profitable unto all things, having promise of the life that now is, and of that which is to come" (1 Tim. 4:7,8).

John's Courage

John the Baptist stands out among Bible characters as a giant in courage. He was not afraid to challenge the Pharisees and Sadducees in his audience and call them a generation of vipers. He demanded that they bring forth fruits as proof of repentance. He anticipated their self-righteous attitude and their prideful way of thinking and told them: "And begin not to say within yourselves, We have Abraham to our father: for I say unto you, that God is able of these stones to raise up children unto Abraham" (Luke 3:8; cf. Matt. 3:9).

Luke reports that John reproved Herod Antipas for having taken his brother Philip's wife, Herodias, and "for all the evils which Herod had done" Luke 3:19). It took great courage for John to tell the ruler of the land, "It is not lawful for thee to have thy brother's wife" (Mark 6:18; cf. Matt. 14:4).

These times of gross immorality and open sinning in which we are living require men of courage who are not afraid to reprove sin in high places and among the affluent and powerful. Doing one's duty in such instances of flagrant wickedness will bring down the wrath of hate-filled enemies upon the conscientious minister. For such pastors, wrought after the pattern of John the Baptist, there are the heartening promises of God's Word.[13]

John's Zeal

Jesus' commendation of John's ministry, "He was a burning and a shining light [lamp]," describes John's exemplary zeal as a witness for the Savior, the Light of the World. The Evangelist John reports: "There was a man sent from God, whose name was John. The same came for a witness, to bear witness of the Light, that all men through him might believe. He was not that Light, but was sent to bear witness of that Light" (John 1:6-8).[14]

John, who believed in Jesus fervently and loved Him, was not the Light, but was a lamp illuminated by the Lord which shone into the lives of sinful human beings, so that they would come to faith in Him and be saved.

The burning which causes the shining is kindled by the Word of God. Thus the Emmaus disciples said after Jesus had disappeared from their sight on Easter evening, "Did not our heart burn within us, while he talked with us by the way and while he opened to us the scriptures?" (Luke 24:32). Similarly today, the zeal for witnessing for Jesus is created by the Word of God.

Annie Johnson Flint has described the function of a lamp shining for Jesus in the following lines of verse:

His lamp am I,
To shine where He shall say;
And lamps are not for sunny rooms,
Nor for the light of day;
But for the dark places of the earth,
Where shame and wrong and crime have birth,
Or for the murky twilight gray

Where shame and wrong and crime have birth,
Or for the murky twilight gray
Where wandering sheep have gone astray,
Or where the lamp of faith grows dim
And souls are groping after Him.
And as sometimes a flame we find,
Clear-shining, through the night
So dark we cannot see the lamp—
But only see the light—
So may I shine, His love the flame,
That men may glorify His name.[15]

John's Success

The Angel Gabriel prophesied that John's ministry would be successful when he told Zacharias: "and many of the children of Israel shall be turn to the Lord their God" (Luke 1:16). That John's appearance as a prophet, his eloquence and message, attracted people from the city of Jerusalem, and from the region near the Jordan River, is related in Mark 1:5 and Matt. 3:5, 6. Many of these people confessed their sins, and were baptized. John's success was not total, however. Jesus spoke of this when He voiced the results of John's ministry: "All the people that heard him, and the publicans, justified God being baptized with the baptism of John. But the Pharisees and lawyers rejected the counsel of God against themselves, being not baptized of him" (Luke 7:29, 30; cf. Matt. 21:31, 32).

Success in spiritual work is something beyond human control, as John pointed out to his disciples regarding the success of Jesus: "a man can receive nothing, except it be given him from heaven" (John 3:27).

Since success in the work of God's kingdom depends upon the intervention of the Holy Spirit working through the Means of Grace, it is comforting to contemplate that the Lord does not require success from His ministers—only faithfulness.

John's Faithfulness

John began his ministry in the Spring of 26 A.D. His active service was less than a year and a half in duration, when he was imprisoned by Herod Antipas. The Forerunner had been in prison about two years when Herod, on the occasion of his birthday, made his foolish promise, confirmed by an oath, that he would give Salome anything she asked for, up to the half of his kingdom. The damsel conferred with Herodias, her mother, and then requested the head of John the Baptist on a platter. Although Herod regretted his rash promise, he ordered a guard to behead the fearless preacher because of the guests who were present and because of his oath. Thus the Forerunner of the Savior became a martyr, one of the noble band of whom the world was not worthy.[16]

John's brief ministry was marked by singular faithfulness. He fulfilled his mission as the Way-preparer of the Messiah, although he realized that his influence was waning, in favor of the Greater One. He considered Jesus' success a gift bestowed from heaven, and he rejoiced that the Bridegroom was claiming His bride, the Church.[17]

Faithfulness is a prime requisite for the minister of Jesus Christ also in these times. Paul, in speaking of ministers as stewards of the mysteries of God, says: "It is required in stewards that a man be found faithful" (1 Cor. 4:2). Jesus, who is in the midst of the seven golden candlesticks (the churches), and holds the seven stars (messengers) in His right hand, directed John the Beloved to write the pastor of the church in Smyrna: "Be thou faithful unto death, and I will give thee a crown of life" (Rev. 2:10c). Moreover, every minister of the Word will want to hear the commendation of his Lord: "Well done, thou good and faithful servant: thou hast been faithful over a few things, I will make thee ruler over many things: enter thou into the joy of thy Lord" (Matt. 25:21).

John, the Voice in the Wilderness

Mark quotes from Malachi 3:1 and Isaiah 40:3 to introduce the ministry of John the Baptist: "Behold I send my messenger before thy face, which shall prepare thy way before thee. The voice of one crying in the wilderness, Prepare ye the way of the Lord, make his paths straight" (Mark 1:2, 3). Luke adds two additional verses from Isaiah: "Every valley shall be filled, and every mountain and hill shall be brought low; and the crooked shall be made straight, and the rough ways shall be made smooth; And all flesh shall see the salvation of God" (Luke 3:5, 6). When a deputation was sent from the Pharisees to interrogate John as to whom he claimed to be, John answered: "I am the voice of one crying in the wilderness, Make straight the way of the Lord, as said the prophet Esaias" (John 1:23).

John's mission was to be the way-preparer for the Savior, the Son of God. He was to prepare for the advent of Christ by proclaiming the Word of God. He was to be a spokesman for the Most High, a voice crying in the wilderness.

John the Baptist spoke in metaphors and picture language: "Fruits of repentance;" "God is able of these stones to raise up children unto Abraham;" "The axe is laid unto the root of the tree;" "He will throughly purge his floor, and gather his wheat into the garner;" "he will burn up the chaff with unquenchable fire;" "Behold the Lamb of God which taketh away the sin of the world." Preachers of the Word today should follow the example of John and preach in concrete rather than abstract language.

John Preached the Law

John's message in the main was the same as that of Jesus when He began His ministry a few months later: "Repent ye, for the kingdom of heaven is at hand" (Matt. 3:2). Compare Matt. 4:17: "From that time Jesus began to preach, and to say, Repent: for the kingdom of heaven is at hand."[18]

To prepare the hearts of his hearers to believe the Gospel and thus enter the kingdom of God, John first preached the Law of God in all severity and warned about the inevitable judgment. He used the Law as a mirror, so that his listeners would recognize their sins, confess them, and receive his baptism for the remission of sins.

It is noteworthy that John knew the nature of the human heart, and that he was aware also of the sins in the lives of the people who came to him. Demanding the "fruits meet for repentance," John counseled the publicans: "Exact no more than that which is appointed you." He told the soldiers: "Do violence to no man, neither accuse any falsely; and be content with your wages" Luke 3:13, 14.

Ministers of Christ should ever be mindful that the Law of God must be proclaimed to prepare for the preaching of the Gospel.[19] Such preaching of the Law must not be done like shooting a scatter gun (a shotgun), but the aim should be for individual hearts of sinners, so that they cannot escape the judgment of the Law, "The soul that sinneth, it shall die" (Ezek. 18:4). A pastor must be aware of what is occurring in the world around him, so that he will preach both against the sins of the times and the sins of which his hearers are guilty.

John Proclaimed the Gospel

Zacharias, the father of John the Baptist, filled with the Holy Spirit, foretold the gospel ministry of his son when he declared that John would "give knowledge unto his people by the remission of their sins" (Luke 1:77).

The content of John's preaching "the baptism of repentance for the remission of sins" is not given in detail. But, it necessarily included the good news that God graciously forgave all sinners for Jesus' sake, and that the remission of sins is bestowed through baptism.

One of the most dramatic moments recorded in all Scripture occurred one day when John saw Jesus coming and said, "Behold the Lamb of God which taketh away the sin of the world" (John 1:29). This apostrophe and statement is John's most notable declaration of the Gospel. It points to Jesus as God's sacrificial Lamb offered for the sin of the world. The "world" stands for all people of the world, just as all sinners are included by John 3:16: "God so loved the *world.*" The word "sin" (singular) is a collective term which stands for every kind of sin and the cumulative sin of mankind.

After declaring that Jesus is the Lamb of God who takes away the sin of the world, John identified Jesus as the eternal Son of the Father, made known to the Forerunner when the Holy Spirit descended upon the Lord at His baptism in the form of a dove (John 1:30-34).

A Gospel statement which is sometimes incorrectly attributed to the Evangelist John instead of to John the Baptist is recorded in John 3:31-36.[20]

Contemplating the statements which reveal that the Gospel predominated in the preaching of the Lord's Forerunner, reminds pastors today that they are chiefly to be preachers of the Gospel, and that the Law must be proclaimed only in preparation for the Gospel. Walther goes so far as to say that a New Testament preacher is really discharging an alien function when he is preaching the Law.[21]

All true Christian preachers are in a sense way-preparers for the Lord Jesus Christ. In this last hour of the world it is imperative that they preach: "Repent for the kingdom of heaven is at hand." Considering the shining example of John the Baptist, devout pastors will pray the Holy Spirit to cast them in the same mold, and yield themselves altogether and only for the glory of their Lord.

May Christ's holy people,[22] who gratefully receive the proclamation of the Gospel, pray for the coming of God's kingdom also to others in the suppliant syllables of a great mission hymn:
Send Thou, O Lord, to ev'ry place
Swift messengers before Thy face,
The heralds of Thy wondrous grace,
Where Thou Thyself wilt come.[23]

Chapter Notes

1. *luchnos* as compared to *phoos* (The Light = Christ. Compare John 8:12: "I am the Light of the world. . .")

2. Cf. Jesus' silent years (Luke 2:52).

3. "He that sent me to baptize with water. . ." (John 1:33).

4. In Acts 14:23 *cheirotoneesantes* refers to choosing elders (pastors) by a show of hands. In Acts 20:28 such elders (pastors) of Ephesus are declared to have been made overseers (bishops, pastors) by the Holy Ghost.

5. See Edersheim, Alfred, *The Temple,* New York, Revell, 1874, pp. 322-331, about the different classes of Nazarites. John was a life-long Nazarite.

6. Some commentators insist that the "locusts" were carob pods. This error has resulted in carobs mistakenly being called "St. John's bread."

7. King Ahaziah recognized the man described by his servants as Elijah because of his hairy garment and leather girdle. (2 Kings 1:8 RSV: "He wore a garment of haircloth, with a girdle of leather about his loins.") Zechariah 13:4 reveals that false prophets would wear "a rough garment to deceive."

8. Acts 1:5 (The tongues of fire on Pentecost were not, however, the judgemental fire prophesied by John the Baptist in Matt. 3:12 and Luke 3:17. The baptism of fire will occur on the Last Day, Cf. 2 Pet. 3:7-12; Rev. 20:15.)

9. No doubt some "scholars" have an explanation of divergent sources for this *apparent* discrepancy.

10. Phil. 1:20.

11. *dikaios* and *hagios*

12. According to Mark 6:20, Herod admired John and enjoyed listening to him. (This, no doubt, "made him exceeding sorry" to yield to Salome's request for his life.)

13. For example Deut. 31:6; "Be strong and of a good courage, fear not, nor be afraid of them: for the Lord thy God, he it is that doth go with thee; he will not fail thee, nor forsake thee."

14. Jesus' tribute is an apropos commentary for the evangelist's statement of verse 8: "He was not that Light, but was sent to bear witness of that Light."

15. *Faith, Prayer & Tract League,* Grand Rapids, Michigan.

16. Hebrew 11:36-38.

17. See John 3:27-30.

18. *The kingdom of God* and *the kingdom of heaven* are synonymous. It is called *the kingdom of heaven* because it is not of this world, as Jesus told Pilate. Moreover, the citizenship of those who are under this rule of God is *in heaven.* "Our conversation [*to politeum*] is in heaven" (Phil. 3:20).

19. See Walther, C.F.W., *The Proper Distinction Between Law and Gospel,* St. Louis, Concordia, 1928.

20. *The King James Version* does not use quotation marks to indicate words spoken. Versions which attribute verses 31-36 to John the Baptist are: *The New Testament in Modern English* (Phillips), *The New International Version,* and *God's Word.*

21. Walther, C.F.W., ibid., p. 405.

22. "The Collect for the Church" speaks thus of believers because, possessing the righteousness of Christ, they are saints (holy people) in the sight of God.

23. *The Lutheran Hymnal,* St. Louis, Concordia, 1941 Hymn No. 506, stanza 1.

SIXTEEN

John in the Worship of Churches Today

According to John the Evangelist (1:29-36), John the Forerunner identified Jesus as "the Lamb of God which taketh away the sin of the world" after He was revealed as the Son of God at His baptism. These words and other Scriptures related to the mission of the Savior's Forerunner have been incorporated in the worship of the liturgical churches.[1]

The Gloria in Excelsis

The *Greater Gloria* is of ancient usage. It is an amplification of the song of the angelic host sung when Jesus was born in Bethlehem. The part of the *Gloria in Excelsis* which is in praise of Christ refers to Him in the words of John the Baptist. It beseeches, "O Lord God, *Lamb of God,* Son of the Father, *that takest away the sin of the world,* have mercy upon us. *Thou that takest away the sin of the world,* receive our prayer." Thus a Christian congregation is led to glorify Christ as the world's Redeemer because of the testimony of John the Baptist and in the concept of his words.

The rubrics of the liturgical churches direct that the *Gloria in Excelsis* always be sung at the celebration of holy communion and on the chief and minor festivals. It may be omitted during penetential seasons, except on the Third Sunday in Advent and on the Fourth Sunday in Lent. It should not be sung on Good Friday or on a Day of Humiliation and Prayer. Ordinarily its place in the service is following the *Kyrie.*[2]

The Agnus Dei

It is thought that the *Agnus Dei* is of Eastern origin, and was introduced into the Western Church in the seventh century.[3] It is an apostrophe addressed to Christ, based on John's testimony that He is the Lamb of God. In the *Agnus Dei* the worshipper confesses faith in Christ, *the Lamb of God who takes away the sin of the world,* and beseeches Him to have mercy upon us and grant us His peace. The *Agnus Dei* is sung preceding or during the distribution of the Lord's Supper.[4]

The Litany

The *Litany* which has come down to our time in the Common Service is one of numerous responsive prayers.[5] In its conclusion there is a petition addressed to Christ, *the Lamb of God who takes away the sin of the world,* praying Him to have mercy upon us and to grant us His peace.

The *Litany* is used as the General Prayer of the Chief Service for Matins, or Vespers, or a Day of Humiliation and Prayer. When the *Litany* is used at Matins or Vespers, it follows at once after the *Canticle*. The *Benedicamus* and the *Apostolic Benediction* immediately follow the *Lord's Prayer* of the *Litany*.[6]

The Benedictus

The Benedictus is the poetic prayer of praise spoken by Zacharias by inspiration of the Holy Spirit at the circumcision of his son, John the Baptist, when his speech was restored. Not only the first part of the poem which praises the Lord God of Israel for having "visited and redeemed His people," are part of the *Canticle*, but also the words which speak about the role of the Forerunner in God's plan of salvation.

The Benedictus is properly used in the worship of Matins during Advent and on the Sundays from Septuagesima until Palm Sunday.[7]

The Proper Preface for Advent

The transition from the Office of the Word in the Order of the Holy Communion begins with the *Preface*. The minister prays: "It is truly meet, right, and salutary that we should at all times and in all places give thanks unto Thee, O Lord, holy Father, almighty, everlasting God." Thereafter follows the *Proper Preface*, i.e., the *Preface* for the day or season of the church year.

The *Proper Preface* for Advent recalls the message and mission of the

Savior's Way-preparer: "Through Jesus Christ, our Lord, whose way John the Baptist prepared, proclaimed Him the Messiah, *the very Lamb of God,* and calling sinners to repentance, that they might escape from the wrath to be revealed when He cometh again in glory. . ."

Scriptures for Advent

The Gospel for the Third Sunday in Advent in the historic pericopes is Matthew 11:2-10. This reading tells that John sent two disciples to to ask Jesus, "Art thou he that should come, or do we look for another?" Jesus sent them back with the assurance that He was indeed the promised Messiah, for he was doing the works which had been prophesied. After John's disciples departed, Jesus praised the Forerunner and identified him as the messenger of Malachi 3:1.[8]

The Gospel appointed in the historic pericopes for the Fourth Sunday in Advent is John 1:19-28. This Scripture records John the Baptist's testimony when interrogators asked him who he was and why he was baptizing. John told them he was not the Christ, but that he had been sent to prepare the way for the Greater One.[9]

A Collect for the Third Sunday in Advent

O Lord Jesus Christ, who at Thy first coming didst send Thy messenger to prepare Thy way before Thee, grant that the ministers and stewards of Thy mysteries may likewise so prepare and make ready Thy way, by turning the hearts of the disobedient to the wisdom of the just, that at Thy second coming, to judge the world, we may be found an acceptable people in Thy sight; who livest and reignest with the Father and the Holy Ghost, ever one God, world without end.[10]

The Day of the Nativity of John the Baptist

Initially a day during the Epiphany season was devoted in the Western Church to celebrate the birth of John the Baptist. After the 24th of December was set for the Nativity of our Lord, the Day of the Nativity of John the Baptist was designated six months earlier, on June 24.[11]

Scriptures for the Nativity of John the Baptist

The Epistle selected for John the Baptist's Day is Isaiah 40:1-5, a prophecy about the voice crying in the wilderness, "Prepare the way of the Lord. . ."[12]

The Gospel selected for this day is Luke 1:57-80 which reports the birth of John, the joyful reaction of the neighbors, the naming of the child at the circumcision, the wonderous restoration of Zacharias's speech, the *Benedictus*, the brief summary about John's growth and his being in the desert previous to his appearance as a prophet for the people Israel.[13]

The Introit for the Nativity of John the Baptist

The voice of him that crieth in the wilderness: Prepare ye the way of the Lord, make straight in the desert a highway for our God.

And the glory of the Lord: shall be revealed.

Ps. It is a good thing to give thanks unto the Lord: and to sing praises unto Thy name, O Most High.[14]

Collects for the Nativity of John the Baptist

O Lord God, heavenly Father, who through Thy servant John the Baptist didst bear witness that Jesus Christ is the Lamb of God, which taketh away the sin of the world, and that all who believe in Him shall inherit eternal life, we humbly pray Thee to enlighten us by Thy Holy Spirit that we may at all times find comfort and joy in this witness, continue steadfast in the true faith, and at last with all believers attain unto eternal life; through the same Jesus Christ, Thy Son our Lord, who liveth, etc.

Almighty God, who through John the Baptist, the forerunner of Christ, didst proclaim salvation, grant that we may know this Thy salvation and serve Thee in holiness and righteousness all the days of our life; through Jesus Christ, Thy Son, our Lord, who liveth, etc.

God, who didst honor this day through the birth of Saint John the Baptist, grant unto Thy people spiritual gladness and direct the minds of all Thy faithful into the way of everlasting life; through Jesus Christ, Thy Son, our Lord, who liveth, etc.[15]

Prayers for the Nativity of John the Baptist
I

O Almighty and Eternal God, who gavest Thine only-begotten Son to be the Light of the world and the Propitiation for our sins, and didst send John the Baptist as a preacher of repentance and a herald of Christ's kingdom, we praise Thee for our deliverance from sin and death secured by the acceptable sacrifice of the Lamb that was slain, and bless Thee for the revelation of Thy tender mercies made in Holy Writ for our comfort and the upbuilding of the holy Christian Church on earth. Grant, we beseech Thee, that we may daily experience Thy goodness in the consolation of Thy Word. Let us by faith obtain the remission of our sins, fill our hearts with praise and our lips with rejoicing, and guide our feet in the way of peace. Vouchsafe unto Thy Church faithful pastors and teachers to bear witness of the Lamb of God which taketh away the sin of the world, that all who believe in Him may not perish, but have everlasting life. Preserve among us and establish everywhere the ministry of the Word for the instruction of the young in sound doctrine, for the conversion of sinners, the comfort of the distressed, and the guidance of the faithful. Incline many devout parents to bring up their sons to become prophets of the Highest, to go before the face of the Lord to prepare His way, to give knowledge of salvation unto His people. Let a host of pious youths grow up and wax strong in spirit, and send them forth as humble but unwavering witnesses of the Light, who shall not count it loss to forego soft raiment and worldly pleasures and goods, and to decrease in the praise of men, if so be that by their ministry Christ increase. Raise up benevolent Christians and men of means, who with prudent counsel and generous gifts will aid in upbuilding those institutions and agencies whereby Thy saving health is made known to all nations. O Thou who inhabitest eternity, whose name is holy, sanctify us by Thy truth, and grant us Thy peace in our time, that we may hereafter praise and glorify Thee, world without end, through Jesus Christ, our Lord.

II

Lord Jesus Christ, Thou Dayspring from on high, we thank Thee that Thou hast visited us to give light to them that sit in darkness and in the shadow of death and to guide our feet into the way of peace. And we beseech Thee, do Thou also rise in our hearts, and prepare us to receive Thee gladly and to trust firmly in Thee, the Savior from sin. Grant that by the instruction of John whom Thou didst ordain as a preacher of repentance and a messenger of the Gospel, we may acknowledge our sins and embrace Thy salvation. Enable us also to bring forth fruits meets for repentance. May we despise the vain pomp and garish attractions of the world, crucify our flesh, and steadfastly resist all temptations to evil. Let us not be like reeds shaken with the wind, but ready to suffer reproach and persecution for Thy name's sake and, if need be, to seal with our blood the witness of the truth. May it please Thee, by the mouth of faithful witnesses to make known Thy saving health to all nations. Endue the ministers of Thy Word with wisdom and power from on high, that they may turn many hearts to Thee. Show us Thy ways, and teach us Thy paths, and grant us, at the appointed hour, a blessed departure, for the sake of Thy suffering and death.[16]

The Gospel for the Festival of the Reformation

The Gospel for the Festival of the Reformation is from Jesus' singular tribute to the character and unique office of the Forerunner, recorded in Matthew 11. The reading consists of only four verses, 12-15.

This Scripture was chosen evidently to compare Martin Luther, the great Reformer, with John the Baptist.[17]

Hymns in the Worship of the Churches

There are numerous hymns which are based upon John the Baptist's dramatic announcement about the redemptive mission of Jesus, John 1:29: "Behold the Lamb of God which taketh away the sin of the world." The following pages reproduce the words and music of these hymns. Included are Advent hymns and hymns designated to be sung to celebrate the Day of the Nativity of the John the Baptist, June 24.

A Profile of John the Baptist

I Lay My Sins on Jesus

7. 6. 7. 6. D.

John 1: 29
Horatius Bonar, 1844

Aurelia
Samuel S. Wesley, 1864

1 I lay my sins on Je - sus, The spot - less Lamb of God;
2 I lay my wants on Je - sus, All ful - ness dwells in Him;
3 I rest my soul on Je - sus, This wea - ry soul of mine;
4 I long to be like Je - sus, Meek, lov - ing, low - ly, mild;

He bears them all and frees us From the ac - curs - ed load.
He heal - eth my dis - eas - es, He doth my soul re - deem.
His right hand me em - brac - es, I on His breast re - cline.
I long to be like Je - sus, The Fa - ther's ho - ly Child.

I bring my guilt to Je - sus To wash my crim - son stains
I lay my griefs on Je - sus, My bur - dens and my cares;
I love the name of Je - sus, Im - man - uel, Christ, the Lord;
I long to be with Je - sus A - mid the heav'n - ly throng

White in His blood most pre - cious Till not a spot re - mains.
He from them all re - leas - es, He all my sor - rows shares.
Like fra - grance on the breez - es His name a - broad is poured.
To sing with saints His prais - es, To learn the an - gels' song. A - men.

98

Behold the Lamb of God!

6. 6. 6. 4. 8. 8. 4.

John 1: 29
Matthew Bridges, 1848, ab., alt.

Ecce Agnus
"Neues Gesangbuch"
Dresden, 1593, ad.

1 Be - hold the Lamb of God! O Thou for sin - ners slain,
2 Be - hold the Lamb of God! In - to the sa - cred flood
3 Be - hold the Lamb of God! All hail, in - car - nate Word!
4 Be - hold the Lamb of God! Wor - thy is He a - lone

Let it not be in vain That Thou hast died!
Of Thy most pre - cious blood My soul I cast.
Thou ev - er - last - ing Lord, Purge out our leav'n;
To sit up - on the throne Of God a - bove,

Thee for my Sav - ior let me take, My on - ly ref - uge
Wash me and make me pure and clean, Up - hold me thro' life's
Clothe us with god - li - ness and good, Feed us with Thy ce -
One with the An - cient of all days, One with the Par - a -

let me make Thy pierc - ed side.
change ful scene, Till all be past.
les - tial food, Man - na from heav'n.
clete in praise, All Light, all Love! A - men.

99

A Profile of John the Baptist

O Christ, Thou Lamb of God

John 1: 29
Christe, du Lamm Gottes
From the German, 1528
Tr., unknown

Irregular

Christe, du Lamm Gottes
Johann Bugenhagen's "Kirchenordnung"
Braunschweig, 1528

O Christ, Thou Lamb of God, that tak-est a-way the sin of the world,
have mer-cy up-on us! O Christ, Thou Lamb of God, that
tak-est a-way the sin of the world, have mer-cy up-on us!
O Christ, Thou Lamb of God, that tak-est a-way the sin of the world,
grant us Thy peace! . . . A - - - - - men.

Lamb of God, Pure and Holy

John 1: 29
O Lamm Gottes, unschuldig
Nikolaus Decius, 1531
Tr., composite

7. 7. 7. 7. 7. 7. 8. 8.

O Lamm Gottes, unschuldig
"Christl. Kirchenordnung"
Erfurt, 1542

1 Lamb of God, pure and ho - - ly, Who on the cross didst suf-fer,
2 Lamb of God, pure and ho - - ly, Who on the cross didst suf-fer,
3 Lamb of God, pure and ho - - ly, Who on the cross didst suf-fer,

Ev - er pa-tient and low - - ly, Thy-self to scorn didst of - fer.
Ev - er pa-tient and low - - ly, Thy-self to scorn didst of - fer.
Ev - er pa-tient and low - - ly, Thy-self to scorn didst of - fer.

All sins Thou bor-est for us, Else had de-spair reigned o'er us:
All sins Thou bor-est for us, Else had de-spair reigned o'er us:
All sins Thou bor-est for us, Else had de-spair reigned o'er us:

Have mer-cy on us, O Je - sus! O Je - sus!
Have mer-cy on us, O Je - sus! O Je - sus!
Thy peace be with us, O Je - sus! O Je - sus! A-men.

A Profile of John the Baptist

Just as I Am, without One Plea

John 6: 37
Charlotte Elliott, 1836

L. M.

St. Crispin
George J. Elvey, 1862

1 Just as I am, with-out one plea But that Thy

blood was shed for me And that Thou bidd'st me come to Thee,

O Lamb of God, I come, I come. A - men.

2 Just as I am and waiting not
   To rid my soul of one dark blot,
   To Thee, whose blood can cleanse each spot,
   O Lamb of God, I come, I come.

3 Just as I am, though tossed about
   With many a conflict, many a doubt,
   Fightings and fears within, without,
   O Lamb of God, I come, I come.

4 Just as I am, poor, wretched, blind;
   Sight, riches, healing of the mind,
   Yea, all I need, in Thee to find,
   O Lamb of God, I come, I come.

5 Just as I am, Thou wilt receive,
   Wilt welcome, pardon, cleanse, relieve;
   Because Thy promise I believe,
   O Lamb of God, I come, I come.

6 Just as I am; Thy love unknown
   Has broken every barrier down.
   Now to be Thine, yea, Thine alone,
   O Lamb of God, I come, I come.

John in the Worship of Churches Today

Christ unser Herr zum Jordan kam   8,7,8,7,8,7,8,7,7   J. WALTHER. 1524

1 { To Jordan came our Lord, the Christ, To do God's pleasure will-ing,
And there was by Saint John baptized, All righteousness ful-fill-ing;

There did He con-se-crate a bath To wash a-way trans-

gres-sion, And quench the bit-ter-ness of death By

His own blood and pas-sion; He would a new life give us.

2 So hear ye all, and well perceive
    What God doth call a Baptism.
And what a Christian should believe
    Who error shuns and schism:

That we should water use, the Lord
    Declareth in His pleasure,
Not simple water, but the Word
    And Spirit without measure;—
He is the true Baptizer.

A Profile of John the Baptist

3 To show us this, He hath His word
  With signs and symbols given;
  On Jordan's banks was plainly heard
  The Father's voice from heaven:
  "This is my well-beloved Son,
  In whom my soul delighteth;
  Hear him!" Yea, hear Him every one,
  Whom He Himself inviteth;
  Hear and obey His teaching!

4 In tender manhood God the Son
  In Jordan's water standeth;
  The Holy Ghost from heaven's throne
  In dovelike form descendeth:
  That thus the truth be not denied,
  Nor should our faith e'er waver,
  That the Three Persons all preside
  At Baptism's holy laver,
  And dwell with the believer.

5 Thus Jesus His disciples sent
  Go, teach ye every nation.
  That, lost in sin, they must repent,
  And flee from condemnation:
  He that believes and is baptized

  Shall thereby have salvation,
  A new-born man he is in Christ,
  From death free and damnation,
  He shall inherit heaven.

6 Who in this mercy hath not faith
  Nor aught therein discerneth,
  Is yet in sin, condemned to death
  And fire that ever burneth:
  His holiness avails him not,
  Nor aught which he is doing;
  His inborn sin brings all to naught,
  And maketh sure his ruin:
  Himself he cannot succor.

7 The eye of sense alone is dim,
  And nothing sees but water;
  Faith sees Christ Jesus, and in Him
  The Lamb ordained for slaughter;
  It sees the cleansing fountain, red
  With the dear blood of Jesus,
  Which from the sins, inherited
  From fallen Adam, frees us,
  And from our own misdoings.

Dr. Martin Luther. 1543   Richard Massie. Tr.

No. 401, Evangelical Lutheran Hymn-Book, Concordia, St. Louis, 1924.

O Jesus, Lamb of God, Thou Art

John 1: 29
O Lämmlein Gottes, Jesu Christ
Bartholomäus Helder, 1646
Tr., August Crull. 1880. alt.

L. M.

Weimar
C. P. Emanuel Bach. 1784

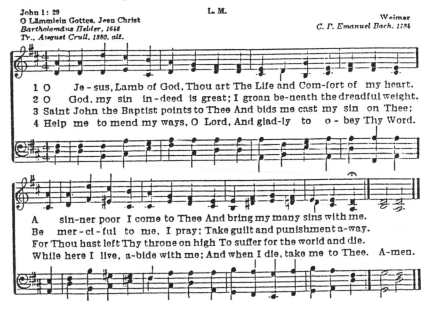

1 O   Je-sus, Lamb of God, Thou art The Life and Com-fort of my heart.
2 O   God, my sin in-deed is great; I groan be-neath the dreadful weight.
3 Saint John the Baptist points to Thee And bids me cast my sin on Thee;
4 Help me to mend my ways, O Lord, And glad-ly to o-bey Thy Word.

A   sin-ner poor I come to Thee And bring my many sins with me.
Be   mer-ci-ful to me, I pray; Take guilt and punishment a-way.
For Thou hast left Thy throne on high To suf-fer for the world and die.
While here I live, a-bide with me; And when I die, take me to Thee. A-men.

Comfort, Comfort, Ye My People

Is. 40: 1-8

Tröstet, tröstet meine Lieben
Johann Olearius, 1671
Tr., Catherine Winkworth, 1863, alt.

8. 7. 8. 7. 7. 7. 8. 8.

Freu dich sehr
"Genevan Psalter," 1551

1 Com-fort, com-fort, ye My peo-ple, Speak ye peace, thus saith our God;
2 Yea, her sins our God will par-don, Blot-ting out each dark mis-deed;
3 Hark, the Her-ald's voice is cry-ing In the des-ert far and near.
4 Make ye straight what long was crook-ed, Make the rough-er plac-es plain;

Com-fort those who sit in dark-ness, Mourn-ing 'neath their sor-rows' load.
All that well de-served His an-ger He no more will see or heed.
Bid-ding all men to re-pent-ance Since the King-dom now is here.
Let your hearts be true and hum-ble, As be-fits His ho-ly reign.

Speak ye to Je-ru-sa-lem Of the peace that waits for them;
She hath suf-fered man-y a day, Now her griefs have passed a-way;
Oh, that warn-ing cry o-bey! Now pre-pare for God a way;
For the glo-ry of the Lord Now o'er earth is shed a-broad,

Tell her that her sins I cov-er And her war-fare now is o-ver
God will change her plain-tive sadness In-to ev-er-spring-ing glad-ness.
Let the val-leys rise to meet Him And the hills bow down to greet Him.
And all flesh shall see the to-ken That His Word is nev-er bro-ken. A-men.

105

A Profile of John the Baptist

On Jordan's Bank the Baptist's Cry

Is. 40: 3; Matt. 3: 3
Jordanis oras praevia
Charles Coffin, 1736, ab.
St. 1–3, tr., John Chandler, 1817
St. 4, 5, tr., unknown

L. M.

Puer nobis nascitur
"Musae Sioniae," VI, 1609

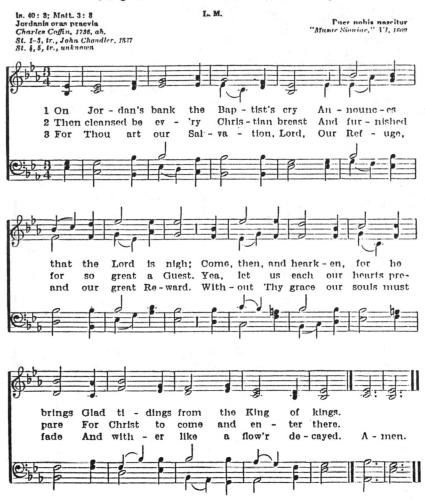

1 On Jor - dan's bank the Bap - tist's cry An - nounc - es
2 Then cleansed be ev - 'ry Chris - tian breast And fur - nished
3 For Thou art our Sal - va - tion, Lord, Our Ref - uge,

that the Lord is nigh; Come, then, and heark - en, for he
for so great a Guest. Yea, let us each our hearts pre-
and our great Re - ward. With - out Thy grace our souls must

brings Glad ti - dings from the King of kings.
pare For Christ to come and en - ter there.
fade And with - er like a flow'r de - cayed. A - men.

4 Lay on the sick Thy healing hand
And make the fallen strong to stand;
Show us the glory of Thy face
Till beauty springs in every place.

5 All praise, eternal Son, to Thee
Whose advent sets Thy people free,
Whom, with the Father, we adore
And Holy Ghost forevermore.

The Nativity of St. John Baptist.

BECCLES.—L.M.   From the Latin, by J.M. Neale

" Behold I will send My messenger, and he shall prepare the way before Me."

mf THE great forerunner of the morn,
The herald of the Word, is born :
And faithful hearts shall never fail
With thanks and praise his light to hail.

With heavenly message Gabriel came,
That John should be that herald's name,
And with prophetic utterance told
His actions great and manifold.

John, still unborn, yet gave aright
His witness to the coming Light;
cr And Christ, the Sun of all the earth,
Fulfill'd that witness at His Birth.

f Of woman-born shall never be
A greater Prophet than was he,
Whose mighty deeds exalt his fame
To greater than a Prophet's name.

mf But why should mortal accents raise
The hymn of John the Baptist's praise ?
Of whom, or e'er his course was run,
Thus spake the FATHER to the SON :

p " Behold My herald, who shall go
Before Thy Face Thy way to show,
And shine, as with the day-star's gleam,
Before Thine own eternal beam."

f All praise to GOD the FATHER be,
All praise, Eternal SON, to Thee,
Whom with the SPIRIT we adore
For ever and for evermore.

A - men.

The Nativity of St. John Baptist.

CROFT'S 148TH.—6 6 6 6 4 4 4 4.

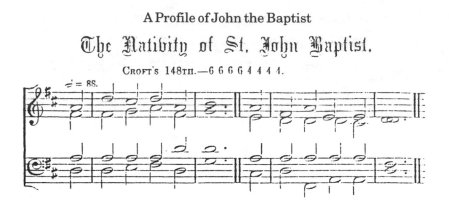

The Nativity of St. John Baptist.

Issac Williams

" Repent ye, for the kingdom of heaven is at hand."

mf LO! from the desert homes,
  Where he hath hid so long,
The new Elias comes,
 In sternest wisdom strong;
cr The voice that cries
  Of Christ from high,
dim And judgment nigh
 From opening skies.

mf Your God e'en now doth stand
 At heaven's opening door;
His fan is in His hand,
 And He will purge His floor;
f The wheat He claims
  And with Him stows,
p The chaff He throws
 To quenchless flames.

f Ye haughty mountains, bow
 Your sky-aspiring heads;
p Ye valleys, hiding low,
cr Lift up your gentle meads;
 Make His way plain
  Your King before.
f For evermore
 He comes to reign.

mf May thy dread voice around,
 Thou harbinger of Light,
On our dull ears still sound,
dim Lest here we sleep in night,
 Till judgment come,
  And on our path
  Shall burst the wrath,
 And deathless doom.

mf O God, with love's sweet might,
 Who dost anoint and arm
Christ's soldier for the fight
 With grace that shields from harm.
f Thrice Blessèd Three,
 Heav'n's endless days
 Shall sing Thy praise
 Eternally.

A - men.

A Profile of John the Baptist

The Natibity of St. John Baptist.

1 By all your saints still striv - ing, for all your saints at rest,
2 *(Insert the stanza appropriate to the day)*
3 Then let us praise the Fa - ther and wor-ship God the Son

your ho - ly Name. O Je - sus for ev - er - more be blessed.
and sing to God the Spi - rit. e - ter - nal Three in One.

You rose. our King vic - to - rious, that they might wear the crown
till all the ran - somed num - ber who stand be - fore the throne

and ev - er shine in splen - dor re - flect - ed from your throne.
a - scribe all power and glo - ry and praise to God a - lone.

Saints' Days.

Words: Horatio Bolton Nelson (1823-1913); ver. *Hymnal 1982*
Music: *Nyland.* Finnish folk melody; adapt. David Evans (1874-1948)

The Nativity of Saint John the Baptist *June 24*

All praise for John the Baptist,
    forerunner of the Word,
our true Elijah, making
    a highway for the Lord.
The last and greatest prophet,
    he saw the dawning ray
of light that grows in splendor
    until the perfect day.

110

When All the World was Cursed

Luke 1: 41
Es war die ganze Welt
Johann G. Olearius, 1697
Tr., Paul E. Kretzmann, 1940

6. 7. 6. 7. 6. 6. 6. 6.

Was frag' ich nach der Welt
Ahasverus Fritsch, 1679

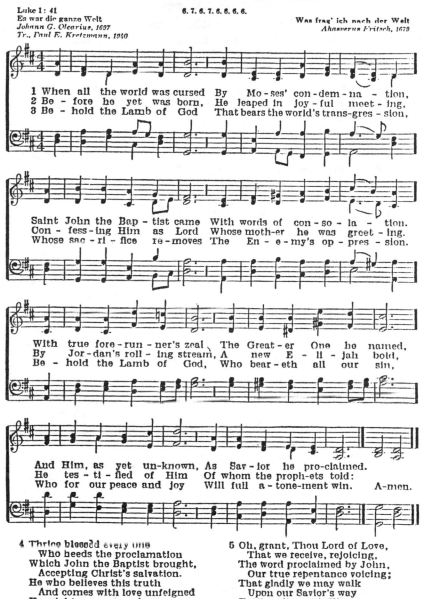

1 When all the world was cursed By Mo-ses' con-dem-na - tion,
2 Be - fore he yet was born, He leaped in joy-ful meet-ing,
3 Be - hold the Lamb of God That bears the world's trans-gres - sion,

Saint John the Bap-tist came With words of con-so-la - tion.
Con - fess-ing Him as Lord Whose moth-er he was greet - ing.
Whose sac - ri - fice re-moves The En - e-my's op - pres - sion.

With true fore-run-ner's zeal, The Great-er One he named,
By Jor-dan's roll-ing stream, A new E - li - jah bold,
Be - hold the Lamb of God, Who bear-eth all our sin,

And Him, as yet un-known, As Sav-ior he pro-claimed.
He tes - ti - fied of Him Of whom the proph-ets told:
Who for our peace and joy Will full a - tone-ment win. A-men.

4 Thrice blessed every one
  Who heeds the proclamation
Which John the Baptist brought,
  Accepting Christ's salvation.
He who believes this truth
  And comes with love unfeigned
Has righteousness and peace
  In fullest measure gained.

5 Oh, grant, Thou Lord of Love,
  That we receive, rejoicing,
The word proclaimed by John,
  Our true repentance voicing;
That gladly we may walk
  Upon our Savior's way
Until we live with Him
  In His eternal day.

Chapter Notes

1. The Eastern Catholic Churches the Roman Catholic Churches, the Anglican and Episcopal Churches, and Lutheran Churches.

2. Webber, *Studies in the Liturgy,* Erie, PA, Ashby Printing Co., 1938, p. 43f.

3. Webber, F.R., op. cit., p. 137.

4. Strodach, Paul Zeller, *A Manual on Worship,* Philadelphia, Muhlenberg Press, 1946, p. 241.

5. Strodach, Paul Zeller, op. cit., p. 290.

6. Strodach, Paul Zeller, op. cit., p. 291.

7. Strodach, Paul Zeller, op. cit., p. 276.

8. For a thorough examination of John's question see our Chapter: *Did John Doubt Jesus' Messiahship?*

9. Some commentators find a difficulty in John 1:24 because the *textus receptus* says, "They that were sent were of the Pharisees." (The priests and Levites were predominantly members of the Sadducee sect. The high priest Annas, according to Joseph *Ant.* XX. 9, 1, was a Sadducee. It has been inferred also from Acts 5:17 that most of the priests and Levites belonged to this sect.) Some scholars think that the *hoi* variant offers a solution, translating, "Some who had been sent belonged to the Pharisees." (This would introduce another interrogating delegation, although the context seems to indicate that the questioning is a continuation of the previous interrogation.) One may assume that the Pharisees mentioned were an exception to the ordinary (predominant) religious persuasion of the priests and Levites.

10. *The Lutheran Liturgy,* St. Louis, Concordia, 1941, p. 52.

11. Horn, Edward T., III, *The Christian Year,* Philadelphia, Muhlenberg Press, 1957, p. 195.

12. The Gospel of Luke, quoting the Septuagint, reproduces the verses which describe the unique mission of the Way-preparer, Mark quotes two verses of Isaiah as compared to one in Matthew's Gospel. In the Fourth Gospel, John identifies himself as the voice in the wilderness described in Isaiah 40.

13. *The Lutheran Hymnal,* St. Louis, Concordia, 1941, p. 91.

14. *The Lutheran Hymnal,* ibid., p. 91.

15. *The Lutheran Hymnal,* ibid., p. 91.

16. *The Lutheran Liturgy,* ibid., p. 377f.

17. Martin Luther truly was a great way-preparer for the Lord, and cast in the mold of John the Baptist.

The Nativity of John the Baptist is celebrated on June 24. The symbol for John the Baptist is that of a Lamb standing on a book. The Lamb is Christ as the nimbus proclaims. The banner is the symbol of His victory over sin, death, and the grave. The book represents the Gospel which John preached.

SEVENTEEN

John the Baptist in Drama

Drama in Medieval Europe had its beginnings in religious observances. One of these was the Feast of Corpus Christi, celebrated on the Thursday after Trinity Sunday. It was a day of colorful processions. These contributed in a large measure to religious drama. Also, the principal feasts of the church year (Christmas, Easter, and Pentecost) were occasions for pageantry. Dramatic skits were presented in the church sanctuary. These plays preceded the later mystery and morality plays. These later dramatic presentations utilized apocryphal writings, legends of the saints, and moral allegories. As secular subjects were introduced and buffoonery, the plays were banned from the church and moved to the open area in front of the church.[1]

John the Baptist was prominent in the Corpus Christi parades, and the story of his life with its dramatic elements became a fascinating subject for mystery plays. Thus the prophet became a popular subject for dramatic presentations in Britain and on the continent.[2]

John the Baptist's unique person, his strong character, his relation to Christ as Forerunner, his unjust imprisonment, the intense hatred of Herodias, and John's grewsome death as a reward for the performance of a dancing girl—all these contributed grist for the mill of playwrights. The following dramas are imaginative expansions of the New Testament account of John's life:

Tragoedia Johannes des Täufers

This tragedy in four acts tells the story of John's life from the beginning until his martyrdom. It was written by Johannes Aal (died 1551) and first published by Mathia Apiario in 1549.[3]

The Baptist

This play was written by George Buchanan (1506-1582), and was republished in 1959 at Edinburgh with *Jephthah* (also by Buchanan). There are only seven actors in this play. A chorus is used with effect by the writer.[4]

Johannis

The dramatist, Friedrich Wilhelm Krummacher, was a pastor of the Reformed church in Germany and a prolific writer of theological works. He is best known for biographical studies of Elijah and Elisha and his most famous book, *The Suffering Savior,* meditations on the last days of Christ.

The drama *Johannis* is remarkable because it was written in 1816 when Krummacher was twenty and a student at the University of Halle. It is a drama of five parts, 288 pages long. These pages reveal an astounding knowledge of the Bible, the details skillfully woven together to sustain the interest of the reader. The delineation of the Savior in the background is a pleasing feature of the play.

As far as we know, this drama has not been translated into English, and it is out of print in German.[5]

Conversion

Nicodemus: Tell me one thing; why do you follow Jesus?
John: It was because of John the Baptist first.
Nicodemus: But why because of him?
John: One day when we were standing by the Jordan,
John and my cousin Andrew and myself,
We saw a man pass by, tall as a spirit;
He did not see us though he passed quite near;
Indeed we thought it strange;
His eyes were open but he looked on nothing;
And as he passed, John, pointing with his finger,
Cried—I can hear him cry it now—
"Behold, the Lamb of God!"

115

Nicodemus: And He, what did He say? What did He do?
John: Nothing; we watched Him slowly climb the hill;
His shadow fell before Him; it was evening.
Sometimes He stopped
To raise His head to the home-flying rooks
Or greet a countryman with plough on shoulder.
Nicodemus: John said, "Behold the Lamb of God?"
John: He said so.
Nicodemus: And from that day you followed Him?
John: No, that was afterwards in Galilee.
Nicodemus: But tell me why; why did you follow Him?
John: I think it was our feet that followed Him;
It was our feet; our hearts were too afraid.
Perhaps indeed it was not our choice;
He tells us that we have not chosen Him,
But He has chosen us. I only know
That as we followed Him that day He called us
We were not walking on the earth at all;
It was another world,
Where everything was new and strange and shining;
We pitied men and women at their business,
For they knew nothing of what we knew—
Nicodemus: Perhaps it was some miracle He did.
John: It was indeed; more miracles than one;
I was not blind and yet He gave me sight;
I was not deaf and yet He gave me hearing;
Nor was I dead, yet me He raised to life.[6]
Andrew Young

Christus: A Mystery

This dramatic poem[7] by Henry Wadsworth Longfellow contains two passages relating to John the Baptist, Christ's Forerunner. The first of these tells about his appearing in the wilderness of Judea. The second passage tells the circumstances of his death. Manahem, an Essene seer cries:

The Prophet of God is dead!
At a drunken monarch's call,
At a dancing woman's beck,
They have severed that stubborn neck
And into the banquet hall

Are bearing the ghastly head!

The passage ends with a curse upon the place where the murder of John the Baptist was contrived and carried out:
Malediction! Malediction!
May the lightnings of heaven fall
On palace and prison wall,
And their desolation be
As the day of fear and affliction,
As the day of anguish and ire,
With the burning and fuel of fire,
In the valley of the Sea!

Salome

Oscar Wilde (O'Flahertie, Wills) (1854-1900) was an Irish wit and playwright. He gained recognition with the novel *The Picture of Dorian Gray* (1891) and comedies such as *Lady Windermere's Fan* (1892), *An Ideal Husband* (1895), and *The Importance of Being Earnest* (1895). His reputation was shattered by his imprisonment for sodomy (1895-1897). During this time he wrote his best known poem, *The Ballad of Reading Gaol.*

Wilde wrote his play, *Salome,* in French in 1893. It was translated into English and published the following year in London and Boston. Although condemned in many quarters as degenerate, the play has been performed in all capitals of the western world more constantly than any other modern English play. It has been translated into thirteen languages.[8] Richard Strauss used it as the basis for his opera *Salome.*

Wilde used the Hebrew form "Jokanaan" for John's name. Salome is portrayed as a young girl in love with Jokanaan. The book jacket of a popular edition of the play describes the play as "A Tragedy of Unrequited Love Turned to Hate."[9] The girl's performance for Herod is described as the dance of the seven veils.

John the Baptist

Hermann Sudermann (1875-1928), a German novelist and playwright was popular among English readers the first part of the twentieth century. This was probably because Sudermann in his literary works protested against social injustice.

John the Baptist (1909) is a long play of five acts with many dramatis personae. As in the play by Oscar Wilde, Salome is attracted

117

to John the Baptist, but spurned by him. The stage directions describe Salome's dance as a salacious performance. John's disciples return in time to tell their master the answer to the question which he had sent them to ask Jesus. After the execution, there is a note of triumph in this that the people in the street are seen waving palms and singing, "Hosannah to the Son of David who comes in the name of the Lord."[10]

John

Philip Barry (1896-1943) was a successful dramatist. His best known work, probably because it was used in a movie, was *The Phildelphia Story*.

The play *John* is a drama in five acts. The first two acts occur in a spacious tent (like a revivalist would use) pitched on the east shore of the Jordan river. John the Baptist is characterized as obsessed with Herod's adultery. He does not appear to know who Jesus really is. That is why he obstensibly sends disciples to ask Him whether He is the Messiah. Herodias offers to help John lead an army of rebellion against the Roman government. John refuses. Unexpectedly, Salome arrives with guards, and they decapitate the courageous prophet.[11]

Chapter Notes

1. See Craig, Hardin, *English Religious Drama of the Middle Ages,* Westport, Connecticut, Greenwood Press, 1978.

2. Anderson, Mary Dèsirèè, *Drama and Imagery in English Medieval Churches,* Cambridge, University Press, 1963.

3. Aal, Johannis, *Tragoedia Johanes des Täufers,* Halle, M. Niemeyer, 1929.

4. Buchanan, George, *Jepthah and the Baptist,* Edinburgh, Oliver and Boys, 1959.

5. Krummacher, Friedrich Wilhelm, *Johannes,* Stuttgart, Herre, 1816. A machine copy of his drama was provided for me by my friend Herr Roland Skerl and through courtesy of the Universitatesbibliothek, Freiburg, Germany.

6. This excerpt from a longer poem, *Nicodemus,* by Andrew Young is from Morrison, James Dalton, editor, *Masterpieces of Religious Verse,* New York, Harper, 1948, p. 242f.

7. Longfellow, Henry Wadsworth, *Complete Poems,* Riverside Press, Cambridge, 1898, p. 468f. & 484 f.

8. Wilde, Oscar, *Salome,* New York, Heritage Press, 1943.

9. Wilde, Oscar, *Salome,* New York, Little & Ives, no date.

10. Sudermann, Hermann, *John the Baptist,* New York, Lane Co., 1909, translated by Beatrice Marshall.

11. Barry, Philip, *John,* New York, Samuel French, 1929.

EIGHTEEN

John the Baptist in Poetry

There are a number of references to John the Baptist in *The Divine Comedy,* by the Italian poet, Alighieri Dante (1265 1321):

> With locusts and the honey of the bee
> The desert has the Baptist fed; and so
> Forever great and glorious is he,
> As in you will the Holy Ghost show.

> And as on this side, with the seats below
> It, does such great division make the place
> Of glory of our Queen of Heaven, so
> Does that of great John opposite it face,
> Who maryrdom and desert's suffering
> And Hell two years, though holy, did endure.[1]

La Vie Saint Jehan Baptiste (author unknown), is a long poem in French composed in the early fourteenth century. It follows the Gospels closely in narrating the life of the Forerunner. A large part of the poem, however, tells about legendary happenings, such as miracles occurring after his death. It also purports to record the various locations to which John's remains were moved. There are some rather lengthy digressions, such as the history of other saints. The poem ends with a resume; a prayer, and a complaint about the current hard times.[2]

> Unholy, sensuous love turns men to beasts—
> A coward, he consented to behead St. John—
> That, for a woman's dance, a woman's song.
>
> *Francois Villon* (1431-1463)[3]

Regis, Joannes, *Parthenandria Prima,* Paris, 1510. The title of this Latin poem suggests the writer's admiration for the celibate life of John the Baptist.[4]

John the Baptist

> The last and greatest herald of heaven's King,
> Girt with rough skins, hies to the desert wild,
> Among that savage brood the woods forth bring,
> Which he more harmless found than man, and mild;
> His food was locusts, and what there doth spring,
> With honey that from virgin hives distilled;
> Parched body, hollow eyes, some uncouth thing,
> Made him appear, long since from earth exiled,
> There burst he forth; all ye whose hopes rely
> On God, with me amidst these deserts mourn,
> Repent, repent, and from old errors turn!
> Who listened to his voice, obeyed his cry?
> Only the echoes, which he made relent,
> Rung from their flinty caves, Repent, Repent!
>
> *William Drummond* (1585-1649)[5]

The Daughter of Herodias
Matthew 14:6

> Vain, sinful Art! who first did fit
> Thy lewd, loath'd Motions unto sounds,
> And made grave Musique like wilde wit
> Erre in loooc airs beyond her bounds?
>
> What fires hath he heap'd upon his dead?
> Since to his sins (as needs it must),
> His Art adds still (though he be dead),
> New fresh accounts of blood and lust.

121

Leave then yong Sorceress; the Ice[6]
Will those coy spirits cast asleep,
Which teach thee now to please his eyes
Who doth thy loathsome mother keep.

But thou hast pleas'd so well, he swears,
And gratifies thy sin with vows:
His shameless lust in publick wears,[7]
And to thy soft arts strongly bows.

Skilful Inchantress and true bred!
Who out of evil can bring forth good?
Thy mother's nets in thee were spread
She tempts to incest, thou to blood.

Henry Vaughan (1622-1695)[8]

O sylvan prophet! whose eternal fame
Echoes from Judah's hills and Jordan's stream,
The music of our numbers raise,
And tune our voices to their praise.

John Dryden (1631-1700)[9]

Messiah

Hark! a glad voice the lonely desert cheers;
Prepare the way! A God, a God appears!
A God, a God! the vocal hills reply;
The rocks proclaim the approaching deity.
Lo, earth receives him from the bending skies!
Sink down, ye mountains, and ye valleys, rise;
With heads declined, ye cedars, homage pay;
Be smooth, ye rocks; ye rapid floods, give way!
The Savior comes! by ancient bards foretold.
Hear him, ye deaf, and all ye blind, behold!
He from thick films shall purge the visual ray,
And on the sightless eyeball pour the day:
'Tis he the obstructed paths of souls shall clear,
And bid new music charm the unfolding ear:
The dumb shall sing, the lame his crutch forego,

And leap exulting like the bounding roe.
                    Alexander Pope (1688-1744)[10]

The Lamb

Little lamb, who made thee?
Dost thou know who made thee?
Gave thee life and bade thee feed
By the stream and o'er the mead;
Gave thee clothing of delight,
Softest clothing, woolly, bright;
Gave thee such a tender voice,
Making all the vales rejoice?
Little Lamb, who made thee?
Dost thou know who made thee?
Little Lamb, I'll tell thee;
Little Lamb, I'll tell thee;
He is called by Thy name,
For he calls himself a Lamb.
He is meek and he is mild,
He became a little child,—
I a child and thou a lamb,
We are called by his name.
Little Lamb, God bless thee.
Little Lamb, God bless thee.
William Blake (1757-1827)[11]

Where is the lore the Baptist taught,
The soul unswerving and the fearless tongue?
The much enduring wisdom sought
By lonely prayer the haunted rocks among?
Who counts it gain His light would wane,
So the whole world to Jesus throng?
                    John Keble (1792-1866)[12]

What Went Ye Out For To See

Across the sea, along the shore,
In numbers more and ever more,

A Profile of John the Baptist

From lonely hut and busy town,
The valley through, the mountain down,

What was it ye went out to see,
Ye silly folk of Galilee?

The reed that in the wind doth shake?
The weed that washes in the lake?

The reeds that waver, the weeds that float?—
A young man preaching in a boat.

What was it ye went out to hear
By sea and land, from far and near?

A Teacher? Rather seek the feet
Of those who sit in Moses' seat.

Go humbly seek, and bow to them,
Far off in great Jerusalem.

From them that in her courts ye saw,
Her perfect doctors of the law,

What is it came ye here to note?—
A young man preaching in a boat?

A prophet! Boys and women weak!
Declare, or cease to rave;

Whence is it he hath learned to speak?
Say, who his doctrine gave?

A prophet? Prophet wherefore he
Of all in Israel's tribes?—

He teacheth with authority,
And not as do the Scribes.

Arthur Hugh Clough (1819-1861)[13]

The Nativity of John the Baptist
Herald of Christ, the day is come,
Day by prophetic lip foretold,
When from the shadow of the tomb
The page of life shall be unrolled:
The daylight dawns; the bright beams glow;
First witness of that light art thou.

Greatest among the sons of clay,
Less than the least in heaven's domain,
Last of the old world, called away
Ere God in man restores his reign:
Thou seest the dawn climb up the skies,
Yet mayest not see the Sun arise.

These beams shall tint the humblest cot,
Shall flood the plains of earth with light,
Thou mayst not feel them: 'tis thy lot
To stand upon the skirts of night:
Didst thou not long to see that morn?
Rejoice: thou seest the daylight dawn.

Through the bright gates of orient pearl
Elias drives his fiery car,
On thee his mantle may unfurl
With spirit and with power from far:
Jordan for thee may part once more,
But earth lies on the farther shore.

'Tis thine in desert paths to stand
And cry, "The Lord's highway prepare!
Heaven's promised kingdom is at hand,
Make straight the rugged pathways there:
Lay low the hills his steps before,
Who comes with fan to purge his floor.

"Upon the hills I hear his feet:
He comes to burn the chaff with fire,
And he will gather in his wheat
Upon the day of wrath and ire;

125

A Profile of John the Baptist

The axe is laid unto the root,
Woe to the tree that bears not fruit!"

Stern accents of the law of fear,
Last threatening accents from above,
Sole birthday in the Church's year
Which wells in death the law of love;
Our God to light for all who die
Brings life and immortality.

Gerhard Moultrie (1819-1861)[14]

John, than which man a sadder or a greater
Not till this day has been of woman born;
John, like some iron peak by the Creator
Fired with the red glow of the rushing morn.
This, when the sun shall rise and overcome it,
Stands in his shining, desolate and fare;
Yet not the less the inexorable summit
Flames him his signal to the happier air.

F.W.H. Myers (1843-1901)[15]

I Went Down Into the Desert
To Meet Elijah

I went down into the desert
To meet Elijah
Arisen from the dead.
I thought to find him in an echoing cave,
For so my dream had said.

I went down into the desert
To meet John the Baptist,
I walked with feet that bled,
Seeking that prophet lean and brown and bold,
I spied the foul fiends instead.

I went down into the desert
To meet my God
By Him be comforted.

John the Baptist in Poetry

I went down into the desert
To meet my God
And I met the devil in red.

I went down into the desert
To meet my God
Oh, Lord, my God, awaken from the dead!
I see you there, your thorn crown on the ground,
I see you there half-buried in the sand;
I see you there, your white bones, glistening, bare,
The carrion-birds a-wheeling round your head.[16]

Vachel Lindsay (1879-1931)[17]

The following is from the book of poetry entitled *He Was Driven Into the Wilderness*. The poem of 43 pages is about the life of Jesus. These verses tell how He came to be baptized.

At dawn he left alone the Jordan road.
He traveled light. His feet were swift and strong.
He slept at night beside the rushing stream.
The second night he was at Jericho,
And hurried eager to the Jordan's ford.
A restless mass of people blocked his way,
But, climbing on a ledge of rock he saw
The prophet at the water's edge, his robe
Discarded, while he took them one by one
Into the stream in solemn pageantry.
The rite continued until darkness fell,
And then the prophet vanished in the night.

The morning dawned upon a cloudless sky.
He saw the prophet coming down the path.
The crowd in wonderment made way for him.
He heard him speak, so near that he could feel
The urgency with which he spoke.
He saw a man of his own age,
Beneath his bearded face and coarse-spun robe,
A man of gentle birth and training in the schools.

A Profile of John the Baptist

When Jesus heard the prophets startling words,
The Christ has come! Unknown as yet, but here!
His shoes I am not worthy to unloose,
Prepare a highway for his sacred feet.
And when he called to them to dedicate
Their lives, he walked into the living stream
To be baptized by John.

Then like a flash of light, the message came.
A voice spoke clearly in his soul, a strong
Compelling voice. You are the one he talks about.
It seemed like thunder in the stillness of
His mind. Amazed, incredulous, he stood
As one struck by a heavy blow is dazed;
And then, unnoticed, disappeared into
The milling crowd and left for Galilee.

Worth Marion Tippy[18]

The following is a stanza from a poem entitled *Darky Sunday School:*

Salome was a chorus girl who had a winning way,
She was the star attraction in King Herod's Cabaret.
Although you can hardly say discretion was her rule,
She's the favorite Bible figure in the Gertrude Hoffman school.

Anonymous[19]

This selection of verse is from a poem with the title *Christ, the Fleur-de-lis:*

Of that beareth witness Saint John
That it was of much renown;
Baptized he was in flom[20] Jordan,
And there-of came the flower delice.[21]
Sing we all, for time it is,
Mary hath borne the flower delice.

Anonymous[22]

See the prize of a dancing girl
The head of a saint for adultery!
See all bloody and glorious
A martyr dies to save chastity.

Anonymous[23]

Also of John a calling and a crying
Rang in Bethabara, till strength was spent,
Cared not for counsel, stayed not for replying,
John had one message for the world, "Repent."

Anonymous[24]

Chapter Notes

1. Dante Aligieri, *The Divine Comedy,* translated from the Italian by Glen Levin Swiggett, Sewanee, TN, University Press, U. of the South, 1956, pp. 303 & 535.

2. *La Vie Saint Jehan-Baptiste,* crit, ed. of an old French poem of the early 14th century, Tübingen, Niemeyer, 1978.

3. Quoted by Bergeaud, Jean, *Saint John the Baptist,* trans. by Jane Wynne Saul, New York, Macmillan, 1961, p. 108.

4. An early published work written in Latin.

5. Drummond, William, included in *Library of Religious Poetry,* ed. Philip Schaff & Arthur Gilman, New York, Dodd-Mead Co., 1882, p. 709.

6. According to legend, Salome fell through the ice, and the ice decapitated her.

7. Salome's dance is believed to have been a lewd exhibition which pleased lustful Herod.

8. Vaughan, Henry, *The Daughter of Herodias,* in *The Mentor Book of Religious Verse,* ed. Horace Gregory and Marya Zaturenska, New York, The New American Library, 1957, p. 82.

9. Dryden, John, *Hymn for the Nativity of John the Baptist,* in *The Catholic Book of Quotations,* ed. John Chapin, New York, Farrar, Strauss & Company, 1956, p. 494.

10. Pope, Alexander, *Poetical Works,* New York, Hurst & Co., 1716, p. 87.

11. Blake, William, *The Portable Blake,* edited by Alfred Kazin, New York, Viking, 1946, p. 85.

12. Keble, John, quoted by F. B. Meyer, *John the Baptist,* Fort

129

Washington, Penna, Christian Literature Crusade, 1975, p. 89.

13. Clough, Arthur Hugh, *What Went Ye Out for to See?*, included in *Library of Religious Poetry*, p. 621.

14. Moultrie, Gerald, *Nativity of John the Baptist, Library of Religious Poetry*, p. 709.

15. Myers, F.W.B., quoted by F.B. Meyer, ibid., p. 9.

16. The poet seems to deny the resurrection of Christ.

17. Lindsay, Vachel, *I Went Down Into the Desert to Meet Elijah*, included in *The World's Great Religious Poetry*, New York, Macmillan, 1923, p. 62.

18. Tippy, Marion Worth, *He Was Driven Into the Wilderness*, Nashville, Abingdon, Parthenon Press, 1960, pp. 12-13.

19. Anonymous, *Darky Sunday School*, included in *The Oxford Book of Verse*, ed. by W.H. Auden, London, Oxford U. Press, 1962, p. 470.

20. *flom* = river.

21. Evidently the poet is giving a transliteration of the French "fleur-de-lis."

22. Anonymous, *Christ, The Fleur-de-lis*, included in *The Mentor Book of Religious Verse, op. cit.*, p. 216.

23. Anonymous. Quoted from *The Grandeur, the Penance, and the Martyrdom of Saint John the Baptist*, by Jean Bergeaud, *Saint John the Baptist*, New York, Macmillan, 1962, p. 108.

24. Author unknown. Quoted by Stewart, James S., *The Life and Teachings of Jesus Christ*, Nashville, Abingdon, no date, p. 34.

NINETEEN

John the Baptist in Music

A previous chapter has noted hymns and portions of the common liturgy related to the life and ministry of John the Baptist used in the corporate worship of Christian churches today. In particular, reference has been made to the theme of John's gospel ministry: Christ, the Lamb of God who takes away the sin of the world. The examples from the liturgy are:

The Gloria in Exceisis
The Agnus Dei
The Benedictus
The Introit for the Nativity of John the Baptist
(Usually sung by the choir)

The hymns sung in the worship of the churches were noted as follows:

I Lay My Sins on Jesus
Behold the Lamb of God
O Christ, Thou Lamb of God
Lamb of God, Pure and Holy
Just as I am Without One Plea
Christ unser Herr zum Jordan kam
O Jesus, Lamb of God, Thou Art
Comfort, Comfort, Ye My People
On Jordan's Bank the Baptist's Cry

A Profile of John the Baptist

*The Great Forerunner of the Morn**
*Lo! From the Desert Homes**
*By All Your Saints Still Striving**
*When All the World Was Cursed**
(*For the Nativity of John the Baptist)

Besides these musical examples, there is a rather large accumulation of other musical works, mostly dramatic, touching the career of the Forerunner. The following works are listed in chronological order:
An ancient hymn which has come down to our time was written by Paul the Deacon about the year 700 A.D. Because each line of the tune started with a different step of the musical scale, Guido of Arezzo (995-1050 A.D.), invented notation and created the sol-fa system of reading notes by syllables using the Latin words of Paul the Deacon's hymn:[1]
UT queant laxis
REsonare fibris
MIra gestorum
FAmuli tuorum
SAlve polluti
LAbii reatum
Sancte Johannes.[2]

A free translation is: "In order that thy servants, with relaxed vocal chords may sing again and again the wonders of thy deeds, absolve our defiled lips from blame, O Saint John."

The following is from an ancient hymn for Matins:
Other prophets could not sing
With heart inspired, the future's Star
But to Him who cleansed the world from sin,
Your finger pointed from far.[3]

Stradella, Alessandro (1639-1682), *San Giovanni Battista, an Oratorio,* Angelicum Recordings, Milan.

Fux, Johann Joseph (1660-1741), *Oratorium Johannes der Täufer,* recorded 1989 by Thorofon, Wedemark, West Germany.

Bonocini Antonio Maria (1677-1726), *La decolliazione di san*

Giovanni Battista (The Beheading of St. John the Baptist), score published New York, Garland, 1986.[4]

Bach, Johann Sebastian (1685—1750), wrote three cantatas for the Day of the Nativity of St. John the Baptist. They are: No. 7. "Christ Unser Herr zum Jordan Kam ("Christ Our Lord Came to the Jordan"), No. 30. "Freue Dich Erlöste Shaar" ("Rejoice Thou Redeemed Multitude"), and No. 167. "Ihr Menschen Rühmt Gottes Liebe" ("You People Extol God's Love"). The theme of John the Baptist's most notable statement of the Gospel comes to mind near the beginning of Bach's *St. Matthew Passion* in the chorale, "O Lamm Gottes unshuldig" ("O Spotless Lamb of God"). And toward the end of his *Mass in B Minor* the "*Agnus Dei*" reminds the hearer of the sacrifice brought to the altar of the cross.

Handel, Georg Friedrich (1685-1759), *Messiah,* libretto by Charles Jennens. After the overture, which introduces the oratorio, a tenor voice sings the first four verses of Isaiah 40. The fifth verse is sung by the chorus. Thus Handel began his masterpiece,[5] *Messiah,* with Isaiah's prophecy of Christ's Forerunner. There is one other verse relative to John the Baptist, the words, "Behold the Lamb of God which taketh away the sin of the world." That is in Part Two where the chorus sings these words to introduce the suffering and death of Christ.

Macfarren, George Alexander, *Saint John the Baptist, an Oratorio,* London, S. Lucas & Co., 1873.

Massanet, Jules Emile Frederic (1482-1912), *Herodiade,* an opera in four acts; libretto by Paul Milliet and Henri Gremont (Georges Hartmann), based on Gustave Flaubert's *Herodias;*[6] which was based on the report of the circumstances of John's death in the Gospels of Matthew and Mark. Massanet's opera was composed upon a more elevated plane than that of Richard Strauss's *Salome.* The sensuality though present is treated with restraint.[7]

Strauss, Richard (1864-1949), *Salome;* libretto by Hedwig Lachmann, based on Oscar Wilde's play. Both the story and music are filled with eroticism. A difficulty encountered in presenting the opera is that a mature voice is required for the role of an immature, teen-age girl.[8]

Chapter Notes

1. See Spaeth, Sigmund, *Stories Behind the World's Great Music,* New York, Garden City, 1940, p. 7f.

2. Note that the hymn is addressed to John as a saint who is regarded able to answer prayer.

3. Quoted by Bergeaud, *Saint John the Baptist,* translated by Jane Wynne Saul, New York, Macmillan, 1962, p. 77.

4. The modern recordings of this and the two preceding works lend evidence for their excellence.

5. *Messiah* is truly the oratorio of all religious dramatic works. It is performed especially during Lent and on Easter Sunday. It is presented not only by professional choruses but by amateur community choirs.

6. Flaubert, Gustave, *Three Tales,* translated from the French by Robert Baldick, London, Penguin, 1961, p. 89ff.

7. Ewen, David, *Encyclopedia of Opera,* New York, Hill & Way, 1963, p. 207.

8. Cross, Milton, *Complete Stories of the Great Operas,* New York, Garden City, 1949, p. 502: "In some productions this is performed by a dancer instead of by the singer."

TWENTY

John the Baptist in Art

John the Baptist's association with Jesus and his unique mission as the Forerunner of the Savior inspired artists to enrich iconography with numerous paintings and sculptures. The astounding epiphany of the Father and of the Holy Spirit at the baptism of Jesus became a favorite subject for medieval artists. It was used in the baptistry of churches and cathedrals. Serial art depicting the life of Christ, whether illustrated in stained glass or otherwise, included scenes related to the ministry of John the Baptist. Even the childhood of Jesus was associated with that of John in the imagination of artists, so that we have him, and sometimes his mother Elisabeth, included in a painting of the Holy Family.

John the Baptist himself, clad in a garment of camel's hair and endowed with the spirit and power of Elijah, was a unique subject for art. In his ministry he appears a heroic figure, censuring the Pharisees for hypocrisy, and condemning King Herod for adultery. He became a tragic hero when his noble head became Salome's prize for a dance.

Symbolism

Almost every portrait of Christ bears some similarity to other representations of Christ. That is, one can usually recognize Him, not only because He is the central figure of a group, but artists have drawn His features in a similar, idealistic way.[1] This phenomenon is not evident in the appearance of John the Baptist in art. His features have little similarity in the portraits of different artists.

The Forerunner is usually pictured as a gaunt and haggard man wearing a garment of animal hair. (The rough cloth woven of camel's hair, was the trademark of his prophetic office.[2]

Sometimes, however, in deference to his noble character and important mission, he is portrayed having a well-developed physique and wearing a scarlet robe.

Paintings of John the Baptist as an infant or young child frequently show him accompanied by a lamb. This was to suggest his mission to proclaim Christ as the Lamb of God who takes away the sin of the world. Also, the iconography which represents the Forerunner as an adult uses a lamb as the motif of his ministry. Sometimes the lamb rests upon a book and suggests that the burden of John's message was the Lamb of God. In a few instances, as for example, in the Isenheim altar-piece, it is the symbol of the wounded lamb whose blood flows into a chalice. The lamb which appears on the shield of John the Baptist, however, bears the cross and a banner of victory. This symbolizes the triumph of the Lamb of God over death in His resurrection from the grave.[3]

The symbol which most frequently indentifies the Forerunner in Christian art is a reed-like staff with a small cross at the top. This symbol appears even in paintings of John as an infant. A modification of this is the staff which John holds in the painting by Francesco del Cossa; there is a small lamb standing within a nimbus (circle) surmounted by a cross.

To the category of symbolism may be added the instances in oriental iconography in which John is represented as an angel. This idea was derived from Malachi 3:1, where the original Hebrew word may be translated either as "messenger" or as "angel."[4]

A disconcerting symbolic personage appears in some paintings of Jesus' baptism in the representation of a "river god" personifying the River Jordan. In some paintings the "river god" is reclining on the bottom of the river; in others he is standing nearby as an observer. Some critics regard this as a pagan intrusion which contradicts the sanctity of the sacred occasion. Other writers in the history of art regard this as mere artistic license which suggests that Jesus' baptism sanctified the waters of the Jordan, which had been used for non-sacred purposes until John the Baptist came baptizing for the remission of sins.[5]

Artistic License

Some artists exercised freedom with the chronology of John's life by portraying him as a mature person along side of the Madonna and Christ-child. Such an adjustment for events related to time is called "an anachronism." Similarly, paintings of Jesus on the cross show John the Baptist pointing to Him and proclaiming Him the Lamb of God who takes away the sin of the world.[6]

An especially strange use of artistic license shows John the Baptist as he appeared in life, either holding his severed head in his hands or with the head separate near by.

Icons

John the Baptist occupies an important place in Eastern Orthodoxy.[7] Accordingly, the Precursor, as he is known in the Greek Orthodox Church, appears frequently in the icons.[8] Icons are the sacred pictures of the Greek Orthodox Church.[9] They are regarded as mystically representing the persons they portray. Icons are venerated as a presence from the invisible heaven made visible.[10] Painted on wood, both sides, they were often carried in processions.[11] In a church they were placed on the inconostasis[12] which served as both a screen separating the apse where the altar stood and as a stand for the icons.[13] The center icon pictured the Savior. On the one side was the icon of the Virgin Mary, and on the other side, on the same level as Mary, the Precursor. Oriental theology does not regard John the Baptist as inferior to Mary in seeking the favor of the Savior.[14] That is why they are presented on the same level in iconography. They are regarded as intercessors. The three figures together form what it called the *Deesis* (the Supplication).[15]

Although the characteristic style of certain schools can be noted, few painters of the icons can be identified because their work is unsigned.[16]

Chapter Notes

1. According to tradition, Luke the Physician, was an artist. Some students of iconography believe that the Chalice of Antioch (The Cloisters, Metropolitan Museum of Art) bears a likeness of Christ copied from a portrait by Luke. It is believed that artists have copied this likeness through the centuries.

2. 2 Kings 1:8.

3. 1 Cor. 15:57: "But thanks be to God, which giveth us the victory through our Lord Jesus Christ."

4. Also the Greek word *aggelos* (Cf. the *Septuagint*) may be translated "messenger" or "angel."

5. See an article in the magazine "Bible Review," February, 1993, pp. 34-41.

6. "The Crucifixion" of the Isenheim altarpiece is a good example.

7. See Danielou, Jean, *The Work of John the Baptist,* Baltimore, Helicon, 1966, p. 144.

8. See Weitzmann, Kurt, *The Icon,* New York, George Brazillar, 1978, p. 7.

9. Rice T. Talbot (Abelson), *Icons,* London, Batchworth Press, 1959, p. 8. Three dimensional art was regarded as "graven images."

10. Danielou, Jean, ibid. p. 144.

11. Rice, T. Talbot, ibid. p. 8.

12. Rice, T. Talbot, ibid. p. 8.

13. Rice, T. Talbot, ibid. p. 8.

14. Danielou, Jean, ibid. p. 145.

15. Weitzmann, Kurt, ibid. page opposite Plate 7.

16. Beginning in the eighteenth century there are icons which have signatures of the artists.

The Madonna of the Chair is one of numerous Madonnas by Raphael Sanzio (1483-1520).This Madonna is popularly repro-duced at Christmas. Reverent little Saint John with folded hands is identified by a faint cross. The original is in the Pitti Gallery , Florence, and is reproduced by courtesy of Fontana Rabatti Domingie/Arte Video.

This *Deesis* is a triptych, 6 13/16 by 18 inches open, 1/2 inch deep, copper and enamel. It is of Russian origin, of the XVII (?) Century. The orginal is in the Art Collection of Bob Jones University, amd is reproduced with the permission of the University. Note that Saint John is equated with Mary.

In the mind of a medieval artist John the Baptist was a member of the Holy Family. This painting by Giuseppe Bottani (1717-1784) is one of the most pleasing presentations of this theme. Note the lamb and the reed cross. Our privilege to reproduce this picture is by courtesy of Bob Jones University.

The Baptism of Christ by Andrea del Verrocchio. Vasari, *Lives of the Artists,* states that young Leonardo da Vinci painted one of the angels of this work. Verrocchio pictures John as a vigorous young man. The reproduction is by courtesy of the Uffizi Gallery & Fontana Rabatti Domingie/Arte Video.

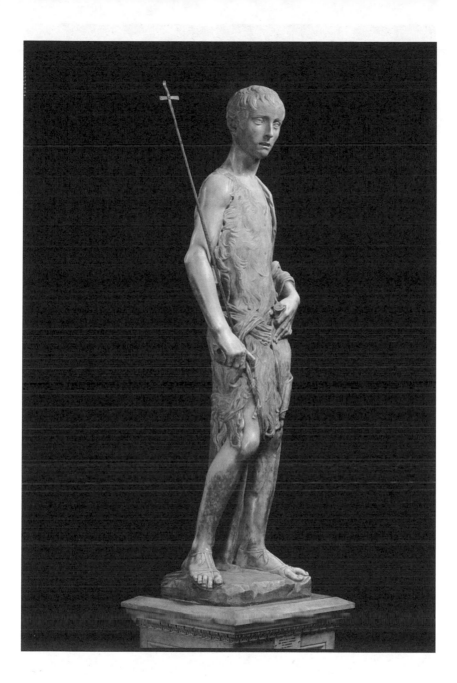

The statue of the youthful Saint John the Baptist is by Desiderio Da Settignano (1426-1468). Note the garment of animal skins and the slender cross, trademarks of the Forerunner. Our photo is by courtesy of the Museo Nationale, Florence, and Fontana Rabatti Domingie/Arte Video.

This picture of young John the Baptist in the desert was painted by the Spanish artist Antonio del Castillo Y Saavedra (1603-1667). The lamb and the cross symbolize John's message of the Lamb of God who takes away the sin of the world. This reproduction is by courtesy of Bob Jones University.

An illuminated page from the Gospel of Hitta (XI Century). This picture of Jesus' Baptism shows an incongruous figure of a river god lurking in the lower right hand corner. The photo has been provided by courtesy of Hessische Landes-und-Hochschul Bibliothek, Darmstsdt, Germany.

Virgin and Child with Saint John the Baptist by Corregio (Antonio Allegro) ,c. 1515, oil on panel (poplar) , 64.2 x 51. cm., Clyde M. Fund, 1965.688.Copyright 1989. The Art Institute of Chicago. All rights reserved. Note the reed cross and the hairy garment which identify the infant John.

August Rodin (1840-1917), the great French sculptor, has formed a John the Baptist full of energy. John is in the act of stepping forward as he speaks and gestures with his right hand. Permission to copy this photo of the bronze statue has been given by the St. Louis Art Museum.

Saint John the Baptist by Francesco del Cossa (c. 1435 -
c. 1477). This is an austere John. Note the unusual staff,
a lamb within a nimbus, surmounted by a cross. The original
painting is in the Brera, Milan, and is reproduced by permission
of the Ministry per i Beni Culturali ed Ambientali.

The statue of John the Baptist at the north portal of Chartres Cathedral is one of the most moving emotionally in all iconography. It speaks of devotion tried by suffering. The shield in his hands depicts a lamb with a cross. The name of the sculptor is unknown. This print is by courtesy of the Cathedral and l'Agence Rapho de Presse Photographique.

The Crucifixion from the Isenheim Altarpiece, 1515, by
Matthias Grunewald, is an example of artistic license in which
the martyred Forerunner points to Christ the Savior. The blood
is pouring into the chalice. This reproduction is by courtesy
of the Unterlinden Museum, Colmar, France, and Service
Photographique.

This is a copy of an icon which pictures Saint John the Baptist as an angel. (The word "messenger' in both Hebrew and Greek may be translated "angel.") The severed head is included by artistic license. The Byzantine Museum, Athens, Greece, has kindly given permission to reproduce the original.

This work, entitled *Sacred Conversation,* by Giovanni di Naccolo
Mansueti, a Venetian (1459-1527), pictures the infant Jesus, the
Virgin Mary, and a mature John the Baptist. The person in the
picture next to the Forerunner is the donor. The other persons
cannot be identified. This reproduction is by courtesy of the Joslyn
Art Museum, Omaha.

French, School of Picardie, 15th Century, Thuison-les-Abbeville Altarpiece: Saint John the Baptist, oil on panel, c.1480, 117 x 52 cm., Mr. Martin A. Ryerson Collection, 1933.1055. Copyright The Art Institute of Chicago. The lamb (with nimbus) reclining on a book is symbolic of John's message of the Lamb of God who takes away the sin of the world.

Salome with the Head of Saint John the Baptist (1639/40) by Guido Reni, oil on canvas, 248.5 x 173.0 cm., Louise B. and Frank H. Woods Purchase Fund 1960.3. This painting is not as gruesome as most artist have concieved the subject. Copyright 1988. The Art Institute of Chicago. All rights reserved.

APPENDIX ONE

Extra-Biblical Sources

Conservative scholars regard the Bible as the inerrant Word of God. Sources of information other than the canonical writings are not regarded as reliable in the sense that God's Word is trustworthy. The Old and New Testaments were written by inspiration of the Holy Spirit. All Scripture is God-breathed.[1] Therefore, the Bible in all its words and thoughts is God's Word, true and reliable.[2] The divine inspiration includes references to secular subjects such as geographical and historical matters.[3] Having declared this, we shall consider extra-Biblical references to John the Baptist.

Flavius Josephus

Josephus tells about the "quarrel" which arose between Aretas, king of Arabia Petrea, and Herod Antipas. Herod was married to the daughter of Aretas. While Herod was in Rome, he fell in love with Herodias, the wife of his brother Philip. He persuaded her to come to live with him, promising to divorce the daughter of Aretas. His wife heard about this intention before Herod knew that she had discovered his plan, and asked to go to Machaerus near the border of her father's kingdom. From that place she fled to her father. The result of Herod's shameful scheme was that Aretas prepared for war against Herod and destroyed his army. Josephus's narrative continues:

"Now some of the Jews thought that the destruction of Herod's army came from God, and that very justly, as a punishment of what he did against John, that was called the *Baptist;* for Herod slew him, who was a good man, and commanded towards one another, and piety towards God, and so to come to baptism; for that the washing [with water] would be acceptable to him, if they made use of it, not in order to the putting away, [or the remission] of some sins [only], but for the purification of the body: supposing still that the soul was thoroughly purified beforehand by righteousness. Now, when [many] others came to crowd about him, for they were greatly moved [or pleased] by hearing his words, Herod, who feared lest the great influence John had over the people might put it into his power and inclination to raise a rebellion, (for they seemed ready to do anything he should advise), thought it best, by putting him to death, to prevent any mischief he might cause, and not bring himself into difficulties, by sparing a man who might make him repent of it when it should be too late. Accordingly he was sent a prisoner, out of Herod's suspicious temper, to Machaerus, the castle I before mentioned, and was there put to death. Now the Jews had an opinion that the destruction of this army was sent as a punishment upon Herod, and a mark of God's displeasure against him."[4]

One should note the following in the report of Josephus: 1. Josephus seems to have drawn some conclusion regarding John's baptism which are untenable on the basis of what the New Testament teaches about baptism. It was not ordained for bodily purification. (See 1 Pet. 3:21.) Also, John did not require that a candidate for baptism would be purified in his soul before receiving baptism. This idea may have originated because John required that candidates for baptism prove that they were sorry for their sins by amending their sinful lives.[5] 2. Josephus informs his readers that John was confined to the castle at Machaerus, something which we would not know otherwise.[6] 3. Also, we learn the name of the daughter of Herodias (Salome) from Josephus.[7]

The Slavonic Josephus

The Slavonic Version of Josephus has been judged as containing additions which are not consistent with the attitudes and historical judgment of the author. *The Slavonic Josephus* does not provide additional information relative to the life of John the Baptist.[8]

The Gospel of Thomas

This work, which purports to have been written by Thomas, the disciple of Jesus, is believed to have been composed in the second century. It contains a collection of 114 sayings of Jesus. There is only one of these (No. 46) which speaks of John the Baptist directly:

"Jesus said, 'Among those born of women, from Adam until John the Baptist, there is no one so superior to John the Baptist that his eyes should not be lowered (before him). Yet I have said, whichever one of you comes to be a child will be acquainted with the kingdom and will become superior to John.'"[9]

There are a number of other sayings of Jesus which may indirectly refer to John the Baptist, but add nothing to what is revealed in the canonical Gospels.[10]

The Gospel of the Ebionites

The Gospel of the Ebionites ("the poor") is extant only because of quotations by Epiphanius.[11] The Ebionites were a heretical Jewish-Christian sect located east of the Jordan River. The statements, apparently, are based upon the canonical Gospels. John's priestly lineage as the son of Zacharias is emphasized. The reference to John's food omits the mention of locusts, probably because the writers were vegetarians.

The Gospel of the Nazareans

Fragments of this work have come down to us in the writings of Jerome. It seems to have been a second century Syriac or Aramaic translation of the Gospel of Matthew.[12] One addition is interesting:

"Behold the mother of the Lord and his brethren said to him: John the Baptist baptizes unto the remission of sins, let us go and be baptized by him. But he said to them: Wherein have I sinned that I should go and be baptized by him? Unless what I have said is a sin of ignorance."

Evidently, it was perplexing to these Christians that the sinless Son of God should receive the Sacrament of Baptism.

The Protevangelium of James

This gospel, written in the middle of the second century, makes the claim that it was written by James, the half brother of Jesus. It appears to have the purpose of exalting the Virgin Mary. It is interesting that Zacharias is designated the high priest.[13] The massacre of the innocents is presented as a threat to the life of the infant John. Zacharias is murdered by servants of Herod, seeking the life of the infant John.[14] His death is linked with the Zacharias mentioned by Jesus in Matthew 23:35.[15] There are other historical errors, so that it adds nothing but absurdities to the authentic record of the canonical Gospels.[16]

Notes for Appendix I

1. *Theopneustos,* 2 Tim. 3:16.

2. 1 Cor. 2:13; 2 Pet. 1:21; John 17:17.

3. See Ramsay, Sir W.M., *The Bearing of Recent Discovery on the Trustworthiness of the New Testament,* London, Hodder and Stoughton, 1915, for numerous examples of how research has proved that Luke is absolutely reliable in referring to secular details.

4. Josephus, Ant. XVIII, V, 2.

5. John required "fruit for repentance."

6. Webb, Robert L., *John the Baptizer and Prophet, A Socio-Historical Study,* Journal for the Study of the New Testament, Itchica, Cornell University Press, 1991, concurs with other recent studies which accept Josephus's passage which speaks of John the Baptist as authentic.

7. Josephus, Ant. XVIII, V, 4.

8. See Steinmann, Jean, *Saint John the Baptist and the Desert Traditionn,* New York, Harper, 1955, p. 132f.

9. Cf. Matt. 11:11.

10. See Webb, op. cit., p. 79f.

11. Webb, op. cit., pp. 81-83.

12. Webb, op. cit., p. 83.

13. Cf. Luke 1:5.

14. Matt. 2:16 gives no indication that the infant John was in danger. The infants in Bethlehem and its environs were sought and slain. It has been estimated that the number was few because of the Bethlehem population at that time. There is no indication that soldiers murdered children of the hill country south of Jerusalem.

15. See 2 Chron. 24:20 for the Zacharis to whom Jesus is referring.

16. See Steinmann, op. cit., p. 134f.

APPENDIX TWO

The Name John

The name John occurs in two forms in Hebrew: *Jehochanan* or *Jochanan*. It means "Jehovah is gracious." Although this name was not represented by anyone in the relationship of Zacharias, it was rather common among the Jews. Eleven men of this name are mentioned in the Old Testament, and three, besides John the Baptist, in the New Testament.[1]

John the Baptist is mentioned a total of 90 times in the New Testament:

23 times in Matthew;
16 times in Mark;
23 times in Luke;
19 times in John;
9 times in Acts.

The Name Saint John

The Bible speaks of those who believe in Jesus Christ as "saints," (holy people).[2] They are righteous in God's sight because they possess Christ's righteousness. "Christ is the end of the law for righteousness to every one that believeth" (Rom. 10:4).

It became a matter of usage that Christians who lived exemplary lives were honored by being called "saints," especially after they had died. As early as the second century there were instances of extraordinary reverence given to "saints," especially martyrs.[3] A number of unscriptural doctrines developed in the course of time, such as the veneration of the saints, praying to them to intercede for human beings, and a dependence upon their supposed treasury of good works for personal salvation.[4] Each medieval country, city, profession, and trade chose its patron saint.[5] Although some of these were removed from the calendar of "saints" in the present century,[6] veneration is still practiced in the Roman and Eastern churches.

Such veneration has also been accorded Saint John the Baptist. He is regarded as the patron saint of Quebec, Canada.[7] Two hundred thirteen villages in France have been named for Saint Jean Baptiste, and the churches which bear his name can hardly be numbered.[8] Numerous famous churches in the cities of Europe are dedicated to him. In the Eastern church, John the Baptist is placed on the same level in the *Deesis* (the supplication) as the Virgin Mary, and receives the veneration of the worshippers.[9]

John the Baptist is considered the Saint of all who pray for the cure of children's diseases. He is regarded as the patron of tanners, saddlers, weavers, tailors, farmers, shepherds, hoteliers, innkeepers, knife-sharpeners, carpenters, musicians and singers.[10]

Monastic Societies Named for John the Baptist

The Order of the Hospital of St. John of Jerusalem (also known as Hospitalers, Knights of Rhodes, and Knights of Malta) was founded as a religious order at the time of the crusades (ca. 1065). The order received a papal charter in 1113 A.D. to minister to sick pilgrims in the Holy Land. It became a military order ca. 1140 A.D. After the fall of Jerusalem it was based in succession on Cyprus (1291), Rhodes (1309), and Malta (1530). The order was expelled from Malta by Napoleon in 1798. Since 1834 the Knights have been established at Rome to carry out their original eleemosynary mission.[11]

Other less known monastic orders which have borne the name of John the Baptist are:

The Penitents of John the Baptist, a Spanish congregation of monks founded in Pamploma during the sixteenth century.[12]

The Barefoot Brotherhood of St. John the Baptist, of the Cloister of Scalzo in Florence, Italy, was founded in the sixteenth century. A series of frescoes on the life of the Forerunner was painted by Andrea del Sarto (1486-1530) for members of this order.[13]

The Cercle Saint-Jean-Baptiste was founded in Paris and Rome, nd has spread to other countries. "Asceticism, contemplation, mission" is their motto.[14]

The Basilian Order of John the Baptist was begun in 1712 by two Syrian monks in a valley near the village of Suwayr in Lebanon.[15]

The Coptic Church and Monastery of John the Baptist was built upon a site near the Jordan River. Since 1967 members of the order have been forbidden to live there because it is in a military area.[16]

The Little Brothers of John the Baptist was founded in this century by Father Leffe, a Belgian Lazarist, as a missionary order among the Chinese.[17]

The Johanniterorden in Germany was disbanded in 1810 by Frederik III of Prussia. It was reactivated in 1852 by his son, Frederik IV, as a Protestant order. Their main activity is education and hospital work.[18]

The Association of Sisters of John the Baptist was founded by Cardinal Zimenes in 1504, but was dissolved in 1835.[19]

The Sisters of John the Baptist and St. Catherine of Siena was founded in 1594 at Genoa, and approved by the pope in 1744.[20]

An order founded by Johanna Maria Baptista Solimani (+1758) for nuns in Moneglia.[21]

Sisters of Saint John the Baptist in Rome was founded at Angri by Magdalena Caputo and Alfonso Maria Fusco. The work of this order is among the youth and in ministering to the sick.[22]

La Societe St. Jean Baptiste

The social, charitable, and cultural Society of St. John was founded in 1834 in Montreal by Ludger Duvernay. It is engaged in secular projects for the advancement of French culture and for improvements in the community.[23]

On June 24 (the Day of the Nativity of St. John) 1874, a universal congress was convened in Montreal of all St. John societies in the Americas. "La Minerve," Montreal's newspaper, lists St. John the Baptist Societies from numerous localities of the United States. Grand banquets were held in Montreal hotels. The advertising pages of the newspaper were filled with announcements of souvenir merchandise.[24]

A current inquiry seems to indicate that only one of the societies in the United States has survived. That is La Societe St. Jean Baptiste de Detroit. A copy of its constitution reveals that the meetings are conducted in French.[25]

Notes for Appendix II

1. Young, Robert, *Analytical Concordance to the Bible,* New York, Funk and Company, 1881.

2. Acts 9:32; Acts 9:41; Rom. 1:7; Rom. 8:27; 1 Cor. 1:2; Phil. 4:12; Eph. 1:1; Col. 1:2; 1 Tim. 5:10; Rev. 19:8.

3. Gibson, George M., *The Story of the Christian Year,* Nashville, Ablingdon-Cokesbury Press, 1945, p. 104f.

4. These "good works" are called works of supererogation in Catholic theology.

5. Attwater, *A Catholic Dictionary,* New York, Macmillan, 1953. See "Patron Saints of Places" and "Patron Saints of Trades."

6. This "purge of saints" occurred in 1969.

7. Bergeaud, Jean, *Saint John the Baptist,* translated by Jane Wynne Saul, New York Macmillan, 1962, p. 90f.

8. Bergeaud, Jean, ibid. p. 85f.

9. Danielou, Jean, *The Work of John the Baptist,* Baltimore, Helicon, 1965, p. 43.

10. Emminghaus, Johannis H., *St. John the Baptist, (The Saints in Legend and Art)* Rechlinghausen, Aurel Bongers, 1967, p. following title page.

11. Williams, Jay, *Knights of the Crusades,* New York, American Heritage, 1962. See pages noted in the index.

12. Eminghaus, Johannes H., ibid., p. 16.

13. Vasari, Giorgio, *Lives of the Aristists,* New York, Simon & Schuster, 1946. p. 235f.

14. Bergeaud, Jean, ibid., p. 85.

15. *The Catholic Encyclopedia,* New York, Catholic U. of America, 1967.

16. *The Coptic Encyclopedia,* New York, Macmillan, 1991, sub. Holy Land, Coptic Churches.

17. Bergeaud, Jean, ibid., p. 84.

18. Meusel, *Kirchliches Handlexikon,* Leitzig, 1891, p. 605.

19. Eminghaus, Johannes, ibid., p. 16f.

20. Lanczkowski, Johanna, *Kleines Handlexikon des Mönchtums,* Stuttgart, Reclam, 1993.

21. Lanczkowski, Johanna, ibid.

22. Lanczkowski, Johanna, ibid.

23. Bergeaud, Jean, ibid, p. 93.

24. Machine copies of "La Minerve" were kindly provided by Louise sier from files of Bibliotheque Nationale du Quebec.

25. The Society of St. Jean Baptiste of Detroit, 3240 Morrissey, Warren, MI 48091.

The Maltese cross of silver on a black field is a symbol for John the Baptist and also for the Order of the Hospital of St. John of Jerusalem.

ARMOIRIES

··· de la ···

Société Saint-Jean-Baptiste de Montréal

RENDRE LE PEUPLE MEILLEUR

Parti: au 1er d'argent à un saint Jean-Baptiste au naturel debout sur une terrasse de sinople; au 2e coupé, au 1er d'azur à trois fleurs de lis d'or, au 2e de gueules à un lion rampant d'or lampassé de gueules.

L'écu timbré d'un castor au naturel et accosté de deux rinceaux d'érable de sinople liés d'argent

APPENDIX THREE

The Day of John the Baptist

Early in the Christian era the custom of observing days in memory of martyrs became customary. The earliest observance for John the Baptist was a day during the Epiphany season of the church. Later, after the birth of Christ began to be celebrated on December 25, the date for the nativity of the Forerunner was set on June 24, six months earlier.[1]

Because it was customary also to celebrate the date of death of martyrs, a second day for observance was established from the time of the Gelasian Sacramentary on August 29, called the Decollation [Beheading] of John the Baptist.[2] Also, "the Annunciation of the Conception of St. John" was celebrated in the fifth century in the Orient, Africa, Gaul, and Spain. June 24, the celebration of the nativity, was regarded among the highest holidays.[3] In the Middle Ages this day was one of holy obligation and a holiday from servile work. The faithful were admonished to attend church. This was the rule in such localities in Germany as Cologne, Treves, Hannover, Hildesheim, Osnabruck, Bavaria, Wurttemburg and Baden.[4] The Day of the Nativity of St. John was also observed as a Christian holiday by Martin Luther,[5] Johann Sebastian Bach,[6] and (in America) by Henry Melchior Muhlenberg.[7]

The Day of John the Baptist is not only a religious holiday, but a day for popular observance in Canada, Europe, and South America. Customs associated with the day are: the St. John's bath, collecting herbs, and the St. John's fire.[8] These customs, associated with the solstice or Midsummer's Eve, were once pagan observances. The bath was connected with benefits believed to be imparted by the natural waters of springs, fountains, streams, and lakes.[9] The herbs were gathered on the eve of St. John's Day to be used as protection against diseases of the mouth.[10] The fires, once lighted by heathen to celebrate the summer solstice, are interpreted as symbolic of John the Baptist whom Jesus described as "a burning and a shining light."[11]

A Catholic cookbook under the heading "Feast of St. John the Baptist" states: "A popular feature of St. John's Day is the celebration of the ancient summer festival of the pre-Christian era. From Scandinavia to Spain, fires are lighted on mountains and hilltops, people gather in the open around a bonfire on the eve of the feast and perform their traditional folk dances. The [Catholic] Church has a special blessing for the 'St. John Bonfire,' and in many places wine is also blessed in honor of the Saint. Various traditional pastries or desserts are eaten on St. John's Day in different sections of Europe. Also, the first products of the spring harvest are served on this day in rural sections of southern Europe."[12]

A current magazine devoted to home furnishings and life in the country brings an article which commends a Scandinavian heritage. The author of the article writes: "Midsummer Eve, the Scandinavian celebration of the solstice and birth of John the Baptist, is a favored picnic date; that warm June evening finds them feasting on pickled herring in mustard sauce, potato salad, Swedish sausage, dark bread, and aquavit—all while the fireflies do their summer dance."[13]

Notes for Appendix III

1. Horn, Edward T., III, *The Christian Year,* Philadelphia, Muhlenberg Press, 1957, p. 195.

2. Horn, Edward T., III, ibid., p. 195.

3. Emminghaus, Johannis H., *St. John the Baptist (The Saints in Legend and Art)* Rechlinghausen, Aurel Bonger, 1967, p. 15.

4. Horn, Edward T., III, ibid., p. 196.

5. The Reformer retained this day and others in the church calendar.

6. Bach wrote at least three cantatas for the Nativity of St. John the Baptist.

7. Muhlenberg conducted church services on this day in 1747. See Horn, Edward T., III, ibid., p. 196.

8. Emminghaus, Johannis H., ibid., p. 19.

9. Emminghaus, Johannis H., ibid., p. 19.

10. Bergeaud, Jean, *Saint John the Baptist,* translated by Jane Wynne Saul, New York, Macmillan, 1962, p. 118f.

11. Emminghaus, Johannis H., ibid., p. 19.

12. Kaufman, William I., *The Catholic Cookbook,* New York, Citadel Press, 1965, p. 201ff.

13. "Country Home," Meredith, Des Moines, June 1994, p. 118.

APPENDIX FOUR

Miscellaneous

The iconography of the life and ministry of John the Forerunner of the Savior is enormous. Several books have been devoted to paintings and sculpture,[1] but they are incomplete because it would be impossible to obtain reproductions of all the art in museums, churches (including cathedrals), and private collections all over the world.

In this profile of John the Baptist we have endeavored only to present representative reproductions to illustrate how artists in their imagination have portrayed him, and the devices and symbolism they have utilized to emphasize his great mission.

Stained Glass

The origin and beginning of stained glass is not known. The use of small pieces of glass to make pictures was anticipated in the mosaics of ancient times.[2] The use of rather large windows filled with stained glass appears to have been the idea of Abbe Suger of St. Denis near Paris.[3] The Cathedrals of Amiens and Chartres followed the Gothic architecture conceived by Suger and the idea gained acceptance throughout Europe.[4]

Because photographs of stained glass windows cannot begin to convey the colors, and because the details are too small to be discerned, we have not attempted to reproduce the numerous examples related to John the Baptist.

The Bosses

A boss is a carving at the intersection of beams or ribs of an arch. The Cathedral of Norwich in England is noteworthy for being rich in roof bosses showing Scriptural subjects. There are about 400 in the nave and transepts alone, not to speak of those in the cloisters and Bauchun Chapel. Quite a large number of these are related to the birth, ministry, and death of John the Baptist. The presence of these bosses has been offered as evidence that the lost mystery plays of the middle ages frequently presented dramas of John the Baptist.[5]

Postage Stamps

In 1952 the tiny nation of Liechtenstein issued a postage stamp imprinted with a painting related to John the Baptist which Andrea del Sarto executed as a fresco of the Scalzo Monastery in Florence. In 1959 Goya's "Holy Family with St. John" was reproduced on a stamp of Spain. Another later series in Spain reproduced "Children of the Shell," which shows the infant Jesus giving John a drink from a shell.[6]

St. John Plates

Some German museums display carved wooden plates showing the severed head of John the Baptist. These "John plates" *(Johannesschüssel)* were carried in processions and used in mystery plays to tell the grewsome death of the prophet.[7]

San Juan Bautista

Christopher Columbus in his second voyage to the new world in 1493 set foot on an island which he named San Juan Bautista in honor of the Savior's Forerunner. Fifteen years later Ponce de Leon changed the name to Puerto Rico ("Rich Harbor").[8]

St. John's Wort

St. John's Wort in a plant native to Europe which has been naturalized in North America, so that it grows in fields and waste land in the United States and southern Canada. Its name arose from the belief that dew collected from it on the morning of St. John's Day was a cure for diseases of the eye.[9] The botanical name is *hypericum perforatum*. The herb is recommended rather frequently in *The Nature Doctor* where it is stated on page 343 that the red dye of St. John's Wort is soluble in oil and that it is more effective in the form of an oil than as a tincture.[10]

Notes for Appendix IV

1. Hurll, Estelle M., *The Life of Our Lord in Art With Some Account of the Artistic Treatment of the Life of St. John the Baptist,* New York, Houghton-Mifflin, 1898.

Masseron, Alexandre, *Saint Jean Baptiste Dans L'Art,* France, Arthaud, 1957.

Plus, R., *Johannes der Täufer in der Kunst,* Colmar, France, 1938.

2. Lee, Lawrence, et al., *Stained Glass,* New York, Crown, 1976, p. 12.

3. Lee, Lawrence, ibid., p. 17.

4. Lee, Lawrence, ibid., p. 72.

5. Anderson, Mary Dèsirèè, *Drama and Imagery in English Medieval Churches,* Cambridge, U. Press, 1963, p. 89ff.

6. Bergeaud, Jean, *Saint John the Baptist,* trans. by Jane Wynne Saul, New York, Macmillan, 1962, p. 114.

7. Hutter, Heribert, *Medieval Stained Glass,* trans. by Margaret Shenfield, New York, Crown, 1964,. p. 50f.

8. Grosvenor, Melville Bell, *America's Historylands,* Washington, D.C., National Geographic Society, 1962.

9. Everett, W.H., *Field Flowers,* Racine, Whitman Publ. Co., 1945, p.21.

10. Vogel, Dr. H.C.A., *The Nature Doctor,* New York, Instant Improvement, Inc., 1994.

Bibliography

Aal, Johannes, *Tragoedia Johannes des Täufers,* Halle, Niemeyer, 1929.

A Catholic Dictionary, New York, Macmillan, 1953.

Aland, Kurt, *Did the Early Church Baptize Infants?,* Philadelphia, Westminster Press, 1963.

Allegro, J.M., *The Dead Sea Scrolls,* Baltimore, Penguin, 1957.

Anderson, Mary Dèsirèè, *Drama and Imagery in English Medieval Churches,* Cambridge University Press, 1963.

Arndt, William, *Bible Commentary St. Luke,* St. Louis, Concordia, 1956.

Auden, W.H., *The Oxford Book of Verse,* London, Oxford University Press, 1962.

Bamm, Peter (pseudo. for Emrich), *Early Sites of Christianity,* New York, Pantheon, 1957.

Barry, Philip, *John,* New York, Samuel French, 1929.

Barton, Peggy, *John the Baptist,* Salt Lake City, Deseret, 1978.

Bergeaud, Jean, *Saint John the Baptist* (trans. Jane Wynne Saul), New York, Macmillan, 1962.

Bettenson, Henry, ed., *Documents of the Christian Church,* New York & London, Oxford University Press, 1947.

Buchanan, George, *Jephthah and the Baptist,* Edinburgh, Oliver and Boyd, 1959.

Chase, Mary Ellen, *The Psalms for the Common Reader,* New York,

Norton Co., 1962.

Craig, Hardin, *English Religious Drama of the Middle Ages,* Westport, Connecticut, Greenwood Press, 1978.

Cross, Milton, *Complete Stories of the Great Operas,* New York, Garden City, 1949.

Danielou, Jean, *The Dead Sea Scrolls and Primitive Christianity* (trans. Salvator Attanasio), New York, Mentor Omega, 1962.

Danielou, Jean, *The Work of John the Baptist,* Baltimore, Helicon, 1964.

Dante, Alighieri, *The Divine Comedy,* Sewanee, TN, University Press, University of the South, 1956.

Davies, A. Powell, *The Meaning of the Dead Sea Scrolls,* New York, Mentor Books, 1956.

Davies, J.G., *The Origin and Development of Early Christian Church Architecture*, New York, Philosophical Library, 1953.

Edersheim, Alfred, *The Temple,* New York, Revell, 1874.

Edersheim, Alfred, *The Life and Times of Jesus the Messiah,* Grand Rapids, Eerdmans, 1886.

Everett, W.H., *Field Flowers,* Racine, Whitman, 1945.

Flaubert, Gustave, *Three Tales,* London, Penguin, 1961.

Franzmann, Martin H., *Follow Me: Discipleship According to St. Matthew,* St. Louis, Concordia, 1961.

Gibson, George M., *The Story of the Christian Year,* Nashville, Abingdon, Cokesburg Press, 1945.

Graystone, Geoffrey, *The Dead Sea Scrolls and the Originality of Christ,* New York, Sheed and Ward, 1956.

Gregory, Horace & Zaturenska, Marya, *The Mentor Book of Religious Verse,* New York, New American Library, 1957.

Grosvenor, Melville Bell, *America's Historylands,* Washington D.C., National Geographic Society, 1962.

Horn, Edward T., III, *The Christian Year,* Philadelphia, Muhlenberg Press, 1957.

Hugh, Joseph Schonfield, *The Lost Book of the Nativity of St. John,* Edinburgh, T. & T. Clark, 1929.

Hurll, Estelle M., *The Life of Our Lord in Art With Some Account of the Artistic Treatment of the Life of John the Baptist,* New York, Houghton-Mifflin, 1898.

Hymns Ancient and Modern, London, 1889.

Jennings, F.C., *Studies in Isaiah,* Neptune, NJ., Loizeaux Brothers, 1966.

Bibliography

Jerimias, Joachim, *Infant Baptist in the First Four Centuries,* London & Philadelphia, Westminster Pres, 1960.

Josephus, (Flavius Josephus), London, Heineman; New York Putnam, 1926-1965.

Jungkuntz, Richard, *The Gospel of Baptism,* St. Louis, Concordia, 1968.

Kazin, Alfred, ed., *The Portable Blake,* New York, Viking, 1946.

Kittel, Gerhard, *Theologisches Woerterbuch Zum Neuem Testament,* trans. Karl L. Schmidt, Vol. II, New York, Harper, 1958.

Koehler, Alford W., *Summary of Christian Doctrine,* revised ed., River Forest, IL, Koehler Publishing Co., 1952.

Koehler, E.W.A., *Summary of Christian Doctrine,* River Forest, IL, Koehler Publishing Co., 1939.

Kraeling, Carl Herman, *John the Baptist,* New York, Scribner, 1951.

Kretzmann, Paul E., *Popular Commentary,* New Testament, Vol. I, St. Louis, Concordia, 1921.

Krummacher, Friedrich Adolph, *Johannes,* Stuttgart, Harri, 1816.

La Vie Saint Jehan-Baptiste, Tubingen, Niemeyer, 1978.

Laetsch, Theo., *The Minor Prophets,* St. Louis, Concordia, 1956.

Lanczknowski, Johanna, *Kleines Handlexikon des Mönchtums,* Stuttgart, Reclam, 1993.

Lawson, James Gilchrist, *Did Jesus Command Immersion?,* Cincinnati, Standard Pub. Co., 1947.

Lee, Lawrence, et al., *Stained Glass,* New York, Crown, 1976.

Lenski, R.C.H., *The Interpretation of St. John's Gospel,* Columbus, Lutheran Book Concern, 1942.

Lenski, R.C.H., *Interpretation of St. Luke,* Columbus, Lutheran Book Concern, 1934.

Lenski, R.C.H., *Interpretation of St. Matthew's, Gospel,* Columbus, Wartburg Press, 1943.

Lightfoot, J.B., *Saint Paul's Epistles to the Colossians and to Philemon,* Grand Rapids, Zondervan, 1976.

Loane, Marcus L., *John the Baptist as Witness and Martyr,* Grand Rapids, Zondervan, 1968.

Longfellow, Henry Wadsworth, *Complete Poems,* Riverside Press, Cambridge, 1898.

Luther, Martin, *A Short Explanation of Dr. Martin Luther's Small Catechism,* St. Louis, Concordia, 1943.

Luther Martin, *Luther's Works,* American edit., Vol. 22, St. Louis,

Concordia, 1957.

Masseron, Alexander, *Saint Jean Baptiste Dans L'Art,* France Arthaud, 1957.

Plus, R., *Johannes der Täufer in der Kunst,* Colmar, France, 1938.

Meusel, *Kirchliches Handlexikon,* Leibzig, 1891.

Meyer, F.B., *John the Baptist,* Fort Washington, PA, Christian Literature Crusade, 1975.

Miller, Kenneth K., *The Gospel According to Isaiah,* Ann Arbor, Cushing-Malley, 1992.

Morrison, James Dalton, ed., *Masterpieces of Religious Verse,* New York, Harper, 1948.

Pfeiffer, Charles, *The Dead Sea Scrolls and the Bible,* Grand Rapids, Baker, 1969.

Pieper, Francis, *Christian Dogmatics,* Vol. II, St. Louis, Concordia, 1951.

Pieper, Francis, *Christian Dogmatics,* Vol. III, St. Louis, Concordia, 1953.

Pope, Alexander, *Poetical Works,* New York, Hurst & Co., 1716.

Ramsay, Sir W.M., *The Bearing of Recent Discovery on the Trustworthiness of the New Testament,* London, Hodder & Stoughton, 1915.

Reed, Luther, D., *The Lutheran Liturgy,* Philadelphia, Muhlenberg press, 1947.

Rice, T. Talbot (Abelson), *Icons,* Batchworth Press, 1954.

Roberts A., & Donaldson, J., editors, *The Ante Nicene Fathers,* New York, The Christian Literature Co., 1890.

Robertson, A.T., *John the Loyal,* Grand Rapids, Baker, 1977.

Robertson, A.T., *Word Pictures in the New Testament,* Vol. V, New York & London, Harper & Brothers, 1932.

Saarnivaare, Uras, *Scriptural Baptism,* New York, Vantage Press, 1958.

Schaff, Philip & Gilman, Arthur, *Library of Religious Poetry,* New York, Dodd & Mead Co., 1882.

Schlink, Edmund, *The Doctrine of Baptism,* St. Louis, Concordia, 1972.

Scobie, Charles, H.H., *John the Baptist,* Philadelphia, Fortress Press, 1964.

Shanks, Hershel, *Understanding the Dead Sea Scrolls,* New York, Random House, 1992.

Sieck, Henry, *Sermons on the Gospels of the Ecclesistical Year,* St.

Louis, Concordia, 1906.

Smith, Joseph, *Doctrine and Covenants & The Pearl of Great Price,* Salt Lake City, Church of Jesus Christ of Latter Day Saints, 1949.

Spaeth, A., *Annotations on the Gospel According to Saint John,* New York, The Christian Literature Co., 1896.

Spaeth, Sigmund, *Stories Behind the World's Great Music,* New York, Garden City, 1940.

Stalker, James, *The Two Johns of the New Testament,* London, Isbister and Co. Limited, 1895.

Steinmann, Jean, *Saint John the Baptist and the Desert Tradition,* trans. Michael Boyes, New York, Harper Brothers 1958.

Stewart, James F., *The Life and Teachings of Jesus Christ,* Nashville, Abingdon, no date.

Strodach, Paul Zeller, *A Manual on Worship,* Philadelphia, Muhlenberg Press, 1946.

Sudermann, Hermann, *John the Baptist,* trans. Beatrice Marshall, London & New York, John Lane Co., 1909.

Tappert, Theodore G., *The Book of Concord,* Philadelphia, Muhlenberg Press, 1959.

The Catholic Book of Quotations, New York, Farrar, Strauss & Co., 1956.

The Catholic Encyclopedia, New York, Catholic University of America, 1967.

The Coptic Encyclopedia, New York, Macmillan, 1991.

The Encyclopedia of Opera, New York, Hill & Way, 1963.

The Hymnal 1982, New York, The Episcopal Church Pension Fund, 1987.

The Koran, trans. George Sale, 8th edit. Philadelphia, Lippincott, 1913.

The Lutheran Hymnal, St. Louis, Concordia, 1941.

The Lutheran Liturgy, St. Louis, Concordia, 1941.

The World's Great Religious Poetry, Caroline Miles Hill ed., New York, Macmillan, 1923.

Vasari, Giorgio, *Lives of the Artists,* New York, Simon & Schuster, 1946.

Vogel, H.C.A., *The Nature Doctor,* New York, Instant Improvement Co., 1994.

Walther, C.F.W., *The Proper Distinction Between Law and Gospel,* trans. W.T. Dau, St. Louis, Concordia, 1928.

Webb, Robert L., *John the Baptizer and Prophet, A Socio-Historical*

Study, Ithica, Cornell University Press, 1991.

Webber, F.R., *Studies in the Liturgy,* Erie, PA, Ashby Printing Co., 1938.

Weitzmann, Kurt, *The Icon,* New York, George Brazillar, 1978.

Wilde, Oscar, *Salome,* trans. Lord Alfred Douglas, New York, Heritage Press, 1945.

Wilde, Oscar, *Salome,* New York, Little & Ives, no date.

Williams, Jay, *Knights of the Crusades,* New York, American Heritage, 1962.

Ylvisaker, John, *The Gospels,* Minneapolis, Augsburg, 1932.

Young, Robert, *Analytical Concordance to the Bible,* New York, Funk & Co., 1881.

Scripture Index

Index
of Names and Subject

A Profile of John the Baptist

Acknowledgments

For their kind helpfulness, my thanks to:
Joan C. Davis, Director of the Art Gallery and Museum of Bob Jones University, Greenville, South Carolina; and
Louise Terrier, Librarian of the Bibliotheque nationale du Quebec, Montreal, Canada.
For providing photo copies for reproduction gratis, my special thanks to:
Myrtali Acheimastou-Potamianou, Director of the Byzantine Museum, Athens, Greece; and
Herrn Bröning, Librarian of the Hessische-Bibliothek, Darmstadt, Germany.
My profound appreciation to Herrn Roland Sckerl, Durmersheim, for copying the drama *Johannis* by Friedrich Adolph Krummacher, and for other valued research in Germany.
My sincere thanks to Christopher Gardiner, Ph.D., my son-in-law, for research in operatic repertoire; and
Cynthia Koch-Gardiner, Ph.D., my daughter, for helpful research in the Library of the University of Michigan.
My unending gratitude to my wife, Lorraine, for her encouragement and supportive resourcefulness.